Sex Like White Trash

A Path to Liberation

FIRST EDITION, JULY 2011
Copyright ©2011 *by A. McKnight and S. Knox*
All rights reserved

The book has been cataloged as follows:
McKnight, A. & Knox, S., [date]
Sex Like White Trash, A Path to Liberation:
a novel by A. McKnight and S. Knox.
— 1st American ed.
ISBN-10: 0983611939
ISBN-13: 9780983611936
1. Psychology & Counseling—Sexuality—Nonfiction.
2. Psychology—Interpersonal Relations—Nonfiction.
3. Sex and Relationships—Sex and Culture—Nonfiction.
I. Title

Book design & photography by Borderline Productions
www.borderlineproductions.com

Printed in the United States of America

SEXUALITY/ LIBERATION/
SOCIOLOGY/ COUPLES/
HUMOR/ MOTIVATIONAL/
INSPIRATIONAL/ CREATIVE/
EMPOWERING/ BETTER SEX/
INTERPERSONAL RELATIONS/
NOT ANOTHER SELF-HELP
BOOK/

LEGALITIES/•

The information in this publication is intended for adults over 18 years of age and is for informational purposes only.

While the authors have made every effort to provide accurate internet addresses and references at the time of publication, neither author assumes any responsibility for errors or for changes that occur after publication. Further, the authors do not have any control over and do not assume any responsibility for other authors or third-party websites or their content.

Your use of the material is solely at your own risk. The authors make no warranty or guarantee regarding the results, completeness or accuracy of the information presented. You should not rely upon the information as a substitute for consultations with a qualified healthcare professional who is knowledgeable about your individual needs.

> **"The worst crime is faking it.**
> Kurt Cobain

The authors are not liable or responsible to any person or entity for any loss or damage, including incidental, special, punitive, consequential or indirect damages, caused or to have been caused (including, but not limited to, liability arising out of negligence, tort, strict liability, copyright or patent infringement) directly or indirectly by or from the information or ideas contained, referenced or suggested in the book or for any errors, misstatements, inaccuracies or omissions in the information or ideas contained in the publication. Read at your own risk and enjoy!

Thank you x-partners, editors, contributors, supporters, teacher and to those who rocked the photo shoot. Without all of you, this book would have never made it into the hands of people searching for more.

THANKS

WHO WE ARE/ •

Growing up between fake boob beach and liposuction land conditioned me to believe that looks meant everything and expressing any type of sexual desire or pleasure is something only trashy people do. A boyfriend once told me "Stop acting like White Trash" when I was vocalizing my pleasure. Sure, I was being loud but wasn't that a good sign?!

My intensity was clearly not permitted in White Suburbia. So for years I tried to squeeze it into a box of perfection. I worked for a Fortune 500 company, got an MBA and acted like all the rest. I was respectful (uptight), smiley (repressed) and nice (hard up). It was not satisfying. The pretentious life bored me. The purists bored me. Mommy's boys bored me.

Then something changed. I changed. I started to see that I could live outside the bubble of illusion. It was at this point of realization that I decided to pack up and leave across country.

What was I doing? Where would I go? Was there life outside California? I had no answers. The only thing I knew was that I felt free.

With this freedom came a strength. I felt womanly, even more so than the day I outgrew my training bra. I had power and was going to use it. You know when you are unstoppable and just can't get enough?! You want to get things done ~ *hella fast.* You want to be seen ~ *by everyone.* You want to take charge ~ *of everything.* There is no holding back when the beauty merges with the beast.

The beast is still making its way into my life and through the process of writing this book I am struck by the amount of determination that I have used to hold it back. I hope you too will have ah-ha moments when you dive into the meat of this book. ~ A. McKnight, *female*

I'm not one for intros so this is going to be short & sweet. I love sex & food. If you do too, read on. ~ S. Knox, *male*

FROM US TO YOU/ •

You can go about life following the rules of society and have mediocre sex or you can veer from the norm and rock the trailer. If you want anything from this book, you can't settle for mediocracy. You have to admit you are sick of your ordinary life. Single, dating or married. It doesn't matter. You have to want something more. There is no reason for you to change your habits if you are not frustrated enough.

FRUSTRATION IS KEY. WITHOUT IT, YOU WON'T MAKE AN EFFORT TO STEP OUTSIDE YOUR REALITY AND ADAPT TO NEW IDEAS.

The people we want reading our book are those who can turn their backs on conventional wisdom and find new ways. Sure this book is about sex but it is also about life. It is about coming to terms with the raw force inside. You might know this force as the animal, predator or inner whore. Whatever you refer to it as, it needs to be expressed.

This is what's so beautiful about the group of people society has labeled as White Trash. As a whole, they don't hold back. They freely express themselves however they feel in the moment. Whether or not you deem their behavior appropriate is not important. The point is they have the key. The key that challenges the trite mentality of society and opens to a rocking sex life.

Using the stereotype of White Trash and referencing the energetic side of sex, we explain how you can liberate your life. We hold a mirror to the human conditioning of society so you can see what is holding you back.

When we talk about *sexual energy* we mean the force behind procreation and the vital energy that flows through you. It is the energy that drives your desires and keeps you wanting more. *Longer, Harder, Better.*

Even when life is working out for you, there is always something more you can do. The greater awareness you have of what you can do to improve your sex life,

the better everything becomes. Your relationships. Your job. Your confidence. E-v-e-r-y-t-h-i-n-g.

Sex is a panacea. What we want is for you to have it like you want it, when you want it and where you want it.

INTRO/•

Sex remains a taboo. All sexual jokes are considered dirty.
Movies with titty shots are rated R. Sex toys are only sold
at adult shops. Society does not give us much room to
enjoy sexual experiences. We have been conditioned to
suppress our sexual desires. This suppression takes
people to internet porn sites, swinger clubs and online
gambling amongst other places. These pastimes are
becoming an addiction.

Instead of going home and having sex like a porn star,
the masses are choosing to sit in front of a television
watching endless shows or in front of a webcam
masturbating to other loners. It is becoming an
acceptable way to live. White Suburbia is under an
illusion that everything is all right.

If you live in a nice house, drive a nice car and have a nice
job, then you have a nice life. Is everything really all that
nice?

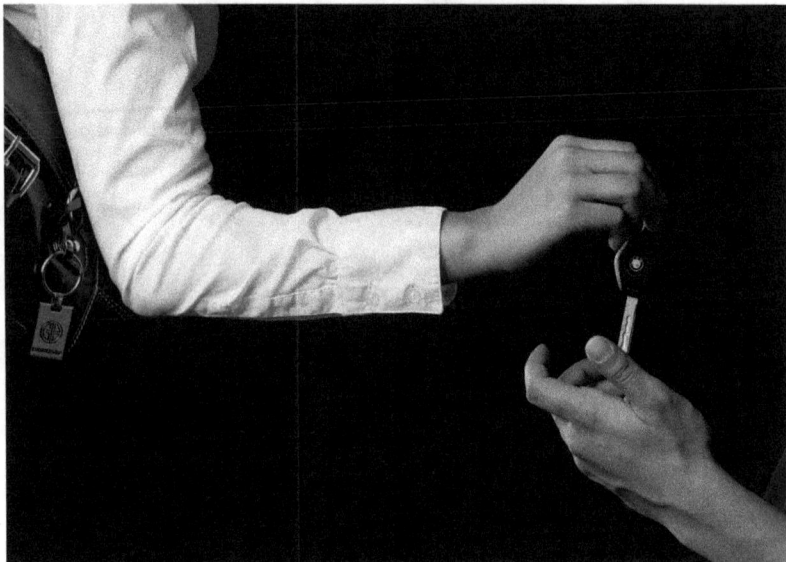

Look at the houses of the 20- and 30-somethings. They are all the same, right out of a fucking Pottery Barn® catalog. Fluffy towels that are too pretty to use. Impersonal art on the walls. Candles that are for display only. Living rooms that are kept too perfect to live in.

As the majority becomes more neurotic, there is one group that remains sane about sex: White Trash. Yes, the mouthy, mullet wearing, WWE watching, duct tape using, park beat-up cars in the grass kind of people. Those who brand themselves with hickeys, Calvin pissing stickers, stone washed jeans and cheap beer. Those who know how to live a life outside the customary rules of society. Those who still have sex often. Shameless sex.

We all have a little White Trash in us. If you are offended by this statement, that's good. It indicates that you are stuck between two worlds. You got this book so you are interested in sex. Yet there is a nagging part that won't let you fully accept it.

A Trojan and StrategyOne survey to measure sexual frequency and satisfaction, finds only about one fifth (21 percent) of respondents are "extremely satisfied" with their sex lives and one in three (30 percent) are generally "dissatisfied." Two-thirds of Americans (62 percent) wish they were having sex more often, while a small number of people report having too much sex (4 percent). Men (73 percent) are more likely than women (53 percent) to want more frequent sex. Further, 76 percent say they are looking for ways to make their sex lives more exciting.[1]

This book aims at talking to the part that is inappropriately slutty. The part that wants to raise the voltage in the bedroom. The part that is crying for more. When reading this book, feel the animalistic side that enjoys raw sex. *Longer, Harder, Better.* Taste the parts that want to be revealed. *Juicy, sweet, nasty.* Feel the waves of sexual desire. *Tingling, soft, intense.* Hear your thoughts like they are holy. *I want sex, I need sex, I love sex.*

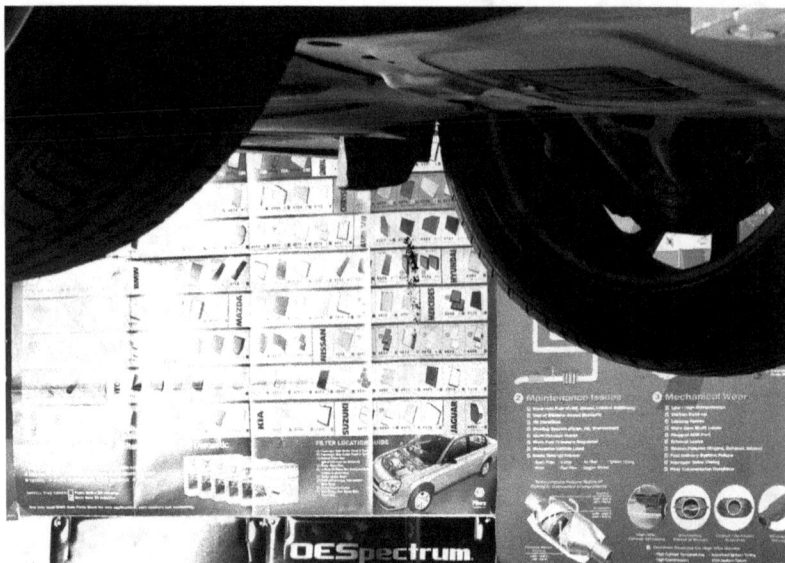

It is freeing to reach a point when you can honor your trashy side and fully incorporate it into your life. Feeling sexual is feeling alive. Look at the people who have a great sex life. They are vibrant. They walk with confidence. They get what they want. Their life rocks. Even if you are one of these people, you can have more.

We approach the topics from a male-female standpoint. However, most of our ideas are just as applicable to gays, lesbians, bisexuals and people of any sexual orientation. If you are a fundamentalist you might as well put this book down and read something less confrontational. We do not advocate cheating, lying or creepy bedroom manners but do question the morals of people who have strict priestly imprints.

When you read in-between the lines, you'll pick up our message which is simple: once you stop conforming to societal norms and conditioning, you can start speaking freely, walking freely and most importantly you can start fucking freely.

AWAKEN THE FORCE/•

Your evolutionary purpose is to have sex. No more advanced than a primate, your existence is meant for breeding and feeding. Instinctively you are drawn to keep your kingdom alive with these two activities. The more you breed, the more you feed. The more orgasms a day, the more your kingdom thrives. The way to stay on top is to be indestructible, like Mike Tyson at his peak.

Though Tyson is a revered fighter, he would have been a legendary all-around hero if he lived centuries ago.

" **My power is discombobulatingly devastating. I could feel his muscle tissues collapse under my force. It's ludicrous these mortals even attempt to enter my realm.**

Mike Tyson

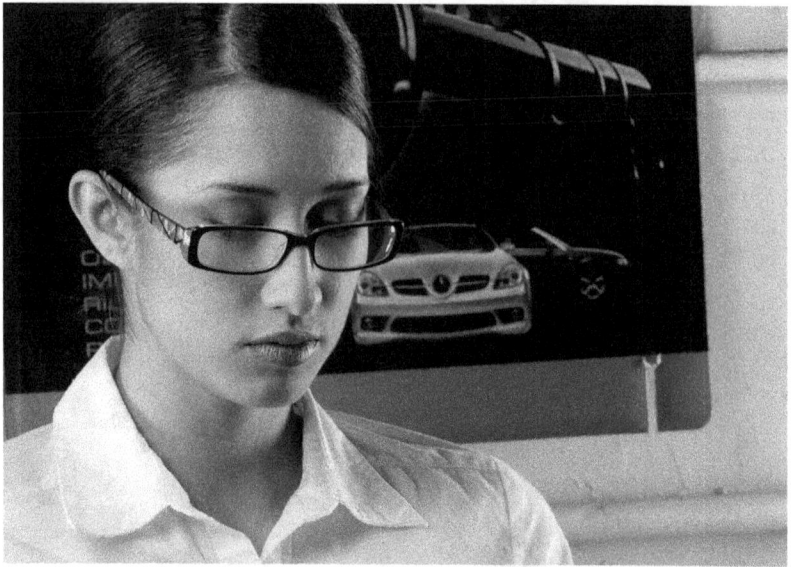

Imagine if his viciousness had been applied to challenge Attila the Hun. He would have conquered countless kingdoms as fast as he took down Michael Spinks. He would have crushed all opposing armies and taken over tribes and harems. He would have been named a god and naked statues would have been sculpted in his honor. Unfortunately, he was born at a time when there are no easy ways for him to express his force other than in the boxing ring.

Nonetheless, you can learn from him. Just look at how he used his power. He was completely unstoppable. His mission was not over until his opponent was lying on the floor destroyed in body and spirit. You have potential for the same strength or you would not have picked up this book. If you don't let it express itself, it is going to eat you alive. You will hate everything. *Maybe you already do.* You will self destruct. *Maybe you are.* Your health will be compromised. *Maybe it is.*

Your Tyson-ness comes from the core or center of gravity, which essentially is the power in your *belly*.

Your belly is where all primordial desires originate, the most fundamental being food and sex. When you are in touch with the desires of your belly, you are feeding the Tyson inside. This makes you powerful in your own way. If you are not in touch with your belly desires, there is nothing to fuel your force. It stays asleep. And when it is sleeping, your life is compromised. Especially your sex life.

Within the past one hundred years, there has been a transition from rural living to urbanization. Instead of being involved in physical activities like farming, people are spending more time at the office in front of a computer. As a result, they are becoming less in touch with their belly. They don't walk, they drive. They don't feel, they think. They don't see, they analyze. All awareness is geared outwards.

For you to truly feel your belly, your awareness needs to be focused inwards. This means moving away from mental activities that draw your attention to outside stimuli to feeling what is going on inside. Forget

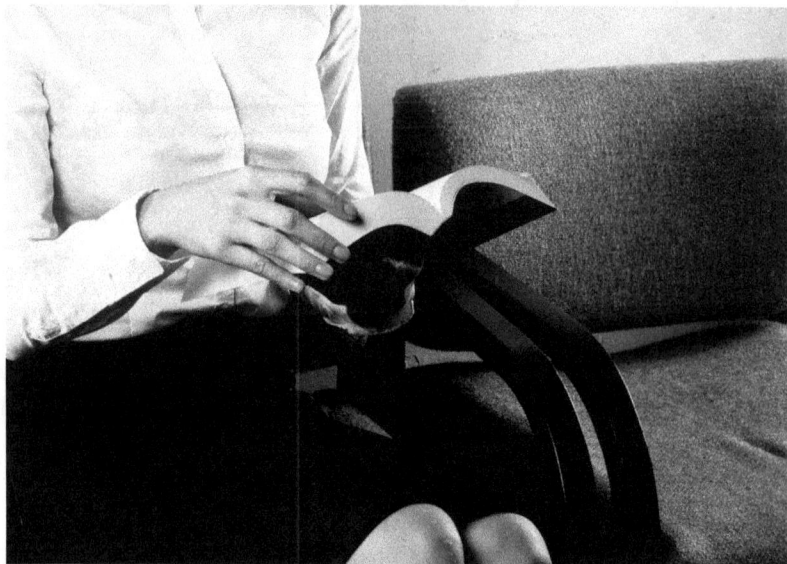

what your mind wants. What does the animal want?

"It's the wanting that keeps us alive."

Paola Franco in *Dangerous Beauty*

Having a gut feeling is being in touch with your belly. It is not something your mind has decided but rather a flash of intuition. Something inside says "Yes" or "No" with complete certainty. The mind might say "*What?!*" but the belly doesn't care. It wants what it wants. There is a natural spontaneity in the belly. It doesn't necessarily make sense but it makes you feel really good. To have this spontaneity is liberating.

The best way to liberate your belly desires is through sex. It is where you can be rough, uncensored and raw. Completely free from appropriate behavior, your force has the chance to awaken. This may bring up sensations you have never felt before like intense desires or violent emotions.

To live out your belly desires doesn't mean you have to get violent. However, you do have to feel your violence. You have to feel it in your belly and perhaps in other areas of your body. This feeling may be perceived as a tingling, pulsing or buzz. Or it may come as a relaxation in your muscles. However you feel it, connect with its intensity. Feel how it makes you alive. It is this awaking that heightens the level of ecstasy and can keep you going like an Energizer Bunny®.

LONGER,

HARDER,

BETTER.

AWAKEN

> "
> YOU AREN'T ALIVE ANYWHERE LIKE YOU'RE
> ALIVE AT FIGHT CLUB.... FIGHT CLUB ISN'T
> ABOUT WINNING OR LOSING FIGHTS.
> FIGHT CLUB ISN'T ABOUT WORDS. YOU
> SEE A GUY COME TO FIGHT CLUB FOR THE
> FIRST TIME AND HIS ASS IS A LOAF OF
> WHITE BREAD. YOU SEE THIS SAME GUY
> HERE SIX MONTHS LATER AND HE LOOKS
> CARVED OUT OF WOOD. THIS GUY TRUSTS
> HIMSELF TO HANDLE ANYTHING.

CHUCK PALAHNIUK
FIGHT CLUB

GETTING INTO YOUR BELLY

1 Sit up straight, making sure your back is not leaning against anything.

2 Relax your whole body, especially your neck and shoulders.

3 Take notice of your breath. Is it shallow or deep? Fast or slow?

4 Put your hands just below your belly button.

5 Take a couple deep breaths. Push your hands out with your breath.

6 Breathe down deep into your belly for two to three minutes.

7 Notice the changes in your body, especially around your belly.

8 You should feel more grounded, a sign that you may be in your belly.

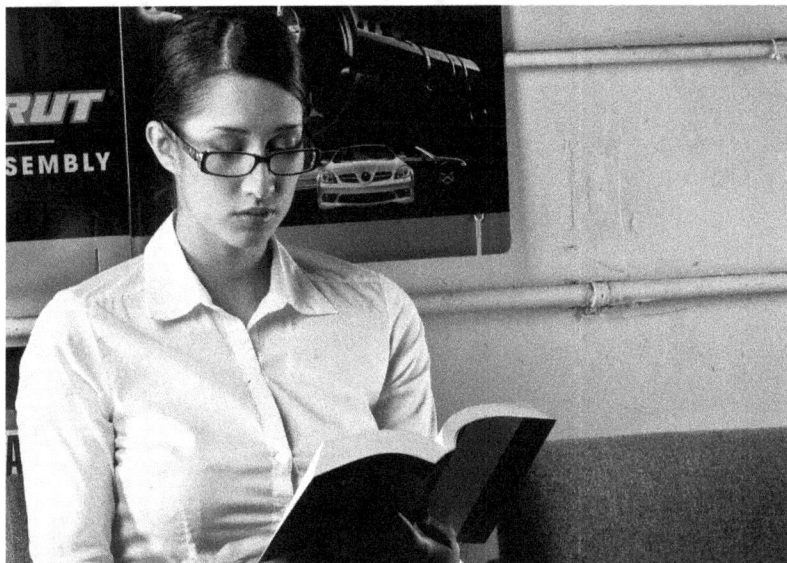

MULTI-CULTI/ •

The place where you grew up heavily impacts your
views on sex. You see sex through the belief systems of
your culture. Local laws reflect your level of tolerance.
You judge people according to your family's scale of
righteousness. In this book the stereotype of White Trash
is used to make this point; however, it can extend to
different memes, groups, organizations and cultures.

Each has its own set of rules, customs and behaviors.
A behavior which is scorned in one place is acceptable
in another. Take a look at Japan. A lot of Japanese
school girls don't have a problem sleeping with business
executives for money. There is no guilt or shame. To
them, it is a great way to make money for their next
shopping spree.

In a religious household, the behavior of these girls is
morally wrong. It is a sin to have sex before marriage.
Only promiscuous girls sleep around outside of wedlock.
And with men twice their age (gasp!). But you see,

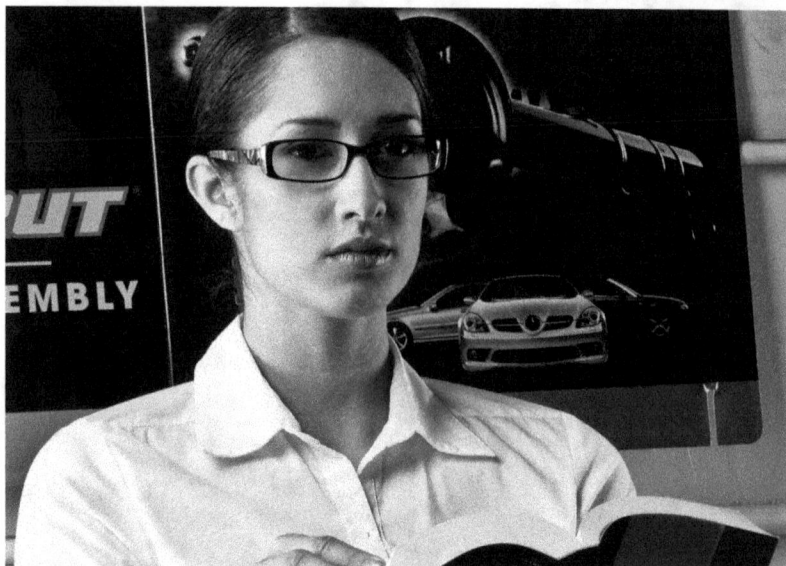

these Japanese girls are not trapped in the same moral dilemma. They enjoy sex without being haunted by ethical judgments. Their culture has shaped their beliefs so they don't have any problem shagging a sugar daddy. Robin E. Brenner in *Understanding Manga and Anime* states "the dark side of the geisha tradition has led to the understanding that older men can buy favors from younger women, usually teenage girls, by acting as sugar daddies. Cautionary tales and joking abound in the manga about this trend - for example, showing teen girls who manipulate older men by granting glimpses of their panties. The more infamous teens seen in *GALS!* and *Confidential Confessions* are the Harajuku girls, named after the district they frequent, who reportedly provide sexual favors to men in return for money to buy designer accessories."[1]

Although sexual desires are natural, sex is wrapped in a lot of guilty connotations, especially in the United States. Brothels are not legal and prostitution is prohibited in most states, which indicates a denial of the reality of sexual desire. Some cultures do not have the same

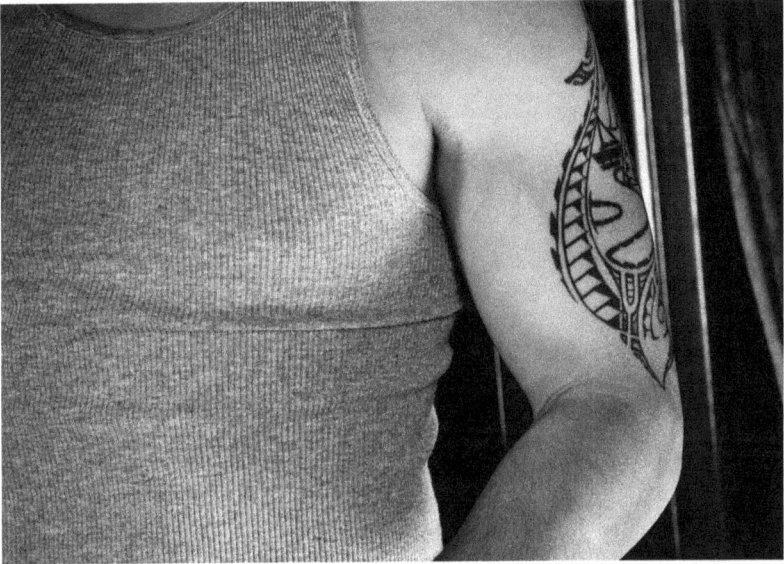

moral-ethical dilemma. Mexican men, for example, are expected to have a sancha, or second lady. A sancha is usually more freaky in bed and does things his wife would not.

In New Guinea, certain tribes encourage pre-pubescent boys to give oral sex to a man at least once a day. Semen is said to contain the essence of masculinity. The boys who want to be the most masculine, therefore, work to ingest as much semen as they can.[2] If you lived in this culture you would not label these young boys as gay or bisexual. You would not label this as child abuse. You would fully embrace the ritual as a natural progression into manhood.

The point is that your view is not really yours.

You have been shaped by your culture. Your parents imprinted the first round of values onto you. They told you what is good and bad, right and wrong. You have been influenced by teachers, religious figures and the media. Your beliefs have been heavily controlled by people like Bill Clinton who defined that oral

copulation is not sex, by Oprah who sparked an interest in a confessional self-help culture and by Homer Simpson. *D'oh*.

All this works unconsciously on your decisions. It does not just include what you think and what you are aware of. It is behind everything you do. It shapes the choice of your partners, the social class you feel a belonging to and the path you take. It merges into every detail of your life from food to furniture, clothes and your vocabulary. It's big!

Fight Club is a great movie that portrays a guy locked up in his cultural beliefs. Playing the devil's advocate, Brad Pitt as Tyler Durden exclaims:

> All the ways you wish you could be, that's me. I look like you wanna look, I fuck like you wanna fuck, I am smart, capable, and most importantly, I am free in all the ways that you are not.[3]

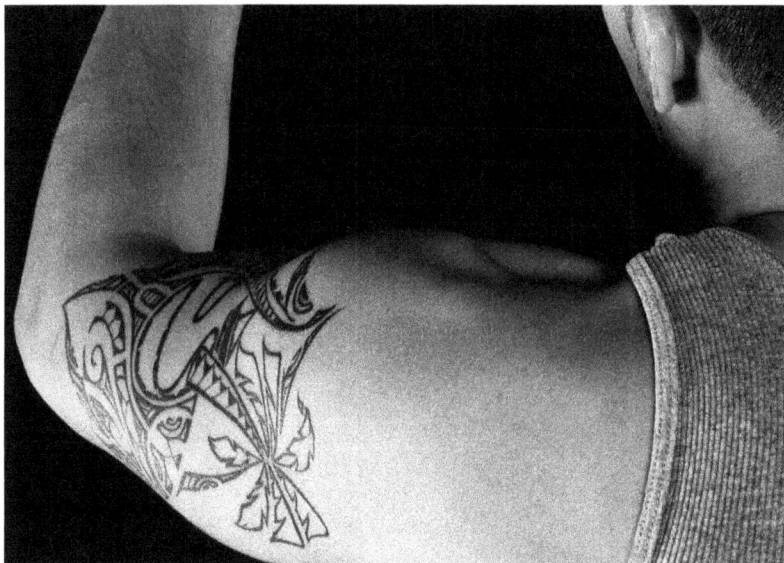

In recognizing that you have adopted societal norms, you liberate yourself from the pressures they place on you. Sure you have to live within certain rules to avoid jail time but you do not have to fully trap yourself in the repression of today's modern world.

The increase in the sadomasochistic sex and bondage scene shows a general disposition for the expression of violence. Often hidden in underground magazines and only accessible through word of mouth, it is stigmatized and ignored in suburban households. But the people who are in touch with their desire have found ways to express themselves. They are not likely to commit acts of sexual violence with partners outside of their grounds. SM aficionados have rules and safe words to create an environment of sexual expression. "Like every other subculture, we have a fringe, an element that doesn't follow the rules," says Susan Wright of the National Coalition for Sexual Freedom, a BDSM advocacy group formed in 1997 that claims 34 member organizations representing 10,000 people. "But every mainstream BDSM group has a mission statement that includes those words over and over: safe, sane, consensual."[4]

> **"PURITANISM: THE HAUNTING FEAR THAT SOMEONE, SOMEWHERE IS HAVING A GOOD TIME.**
>
> H.L. MENCKEN

When you take away the unacceptable behaviors and moral beliefs underpinning the laws of different countries, you are left with people who are no more refined than chimpanzees. They wrap their behaviors and beliefs differently but the underlying sexual desire is there regardless of their culture.

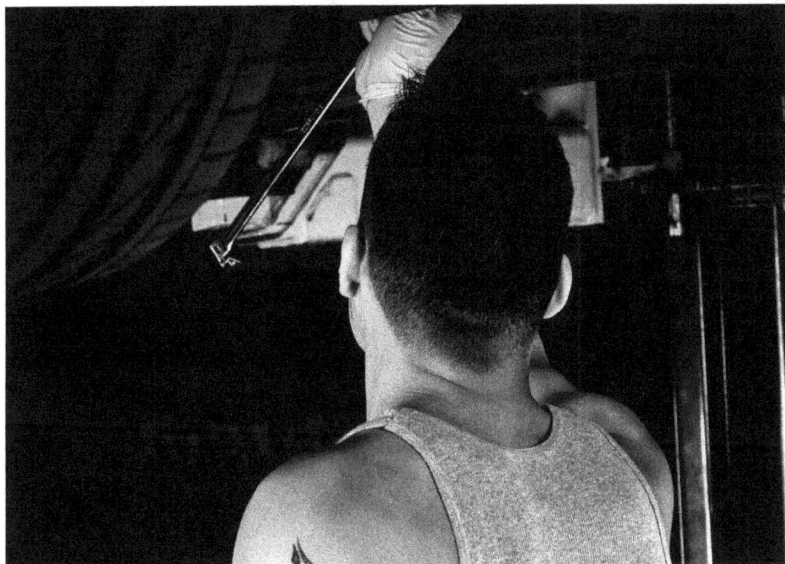

SIN-SATIONAL/ •

What do you fantasize about? Having a threesome in
the storage closet at work? Getting it on with the UPS
delivery person? Dominating a stranger while dripping
hot candle wax on his or her body? ... What nasty
thoughts run through your head that make you a sinner?

Tapping into your fantasies facilitates a healthy attitude to
common desires. Fantasies are part of the human psyche
and everyone has them. The difference is that some
people push fantasies out of their consciousness and
others are brave enough to fulfill them. The former are
the type of people who end up rigid and unsatisfied and
the latter have a well-balanced sex life. It is ironic that
society sees it the other way around.

Society deems fantasies as immoral, dirty and forbidden.
Though, try as it may, society can't stop people from
having them. The signs are everywhere, from mass
produced French maid uniforms to genres on porn sites
to a wide variety of sex toys. Fantasies are universal

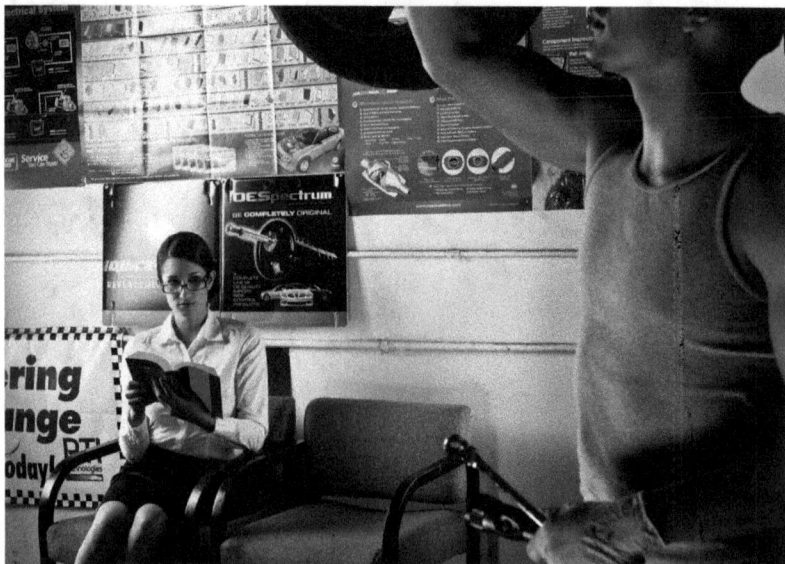

and play a big part in sexual expression. In his book *Who's Been Sleeping in Your Head? The Secret World of Sexual Fantasies*, Brett Kahr, a British psychotherapist, reports on his extensive research in the nonclinical world and concludes that even the most disturbing, frightening fantasies exist in the heads of people who are living healthy, successful lives.[1]

Other authors, like Nancy Friday, have also revealed that fantasies about group sex, incest, homosexuality, bestiality, infidelity and other behaviors exist in every echelon.

WAKE UP

White Trash aren't the only ones preoccupied with sin-sational thoughts.

One common prejudgment is that fantasies have to include leather and whips. If this is what it takes for you to get into your fantasies, great. But you don't need to be a sadomasochist to play out your deepest desires. Simple ones can get you ticking, even if they are not centered around sex.

However, sexual fantasies reach the core. They are wrapped around your deepest desires. They are what keep you occupied, consciously or unconsciously. They consume your thoughts like a hundred little devils sitting on your shoulder. These devils don't care if you are in an important business meeting. All they want is for you to see that the HOPA (hot piece of ass) sitting across from you is a good fuck. You know, they are right. And the more you push these devils away, the harder they fight back. You can hold on tight to your saintly beliefs but if you don't come to terms with your fantasies, you will be easily controlled by these guys. Gaining control means you have to admit that you truly want to do the HOPA right there on the table. *Long and hard.*

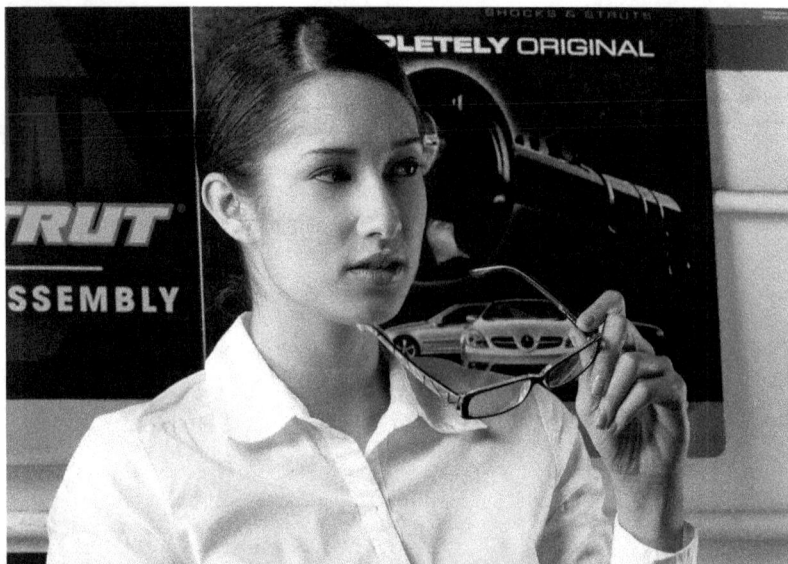

"Sex didn't feel like enough and no emotions were really enough. Nothing really felt like it was (sigh). I didn't feel (sigh). There was always something I wanted to break out of. Feel more connected to another person. Something more honest. And in kinda a moment of wanting to find something honest, I grabbed a knife and cut him [my boyfriend]. He cut me back. We had this exchange of something. Somehow covered in blood, feeling, my heart was racing and there was something dangerous and alive. I suddenly felt more honest."[2] Angelina Jolie

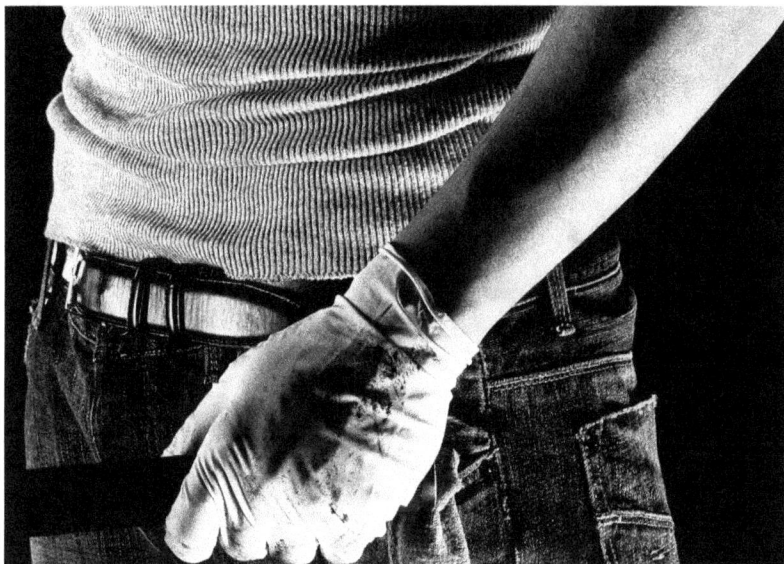

Exploring your fantasies can open doors to the path of liberation. Creating excitement from the inside out, fantasies wake up the hibernating animal that wants to mate and fornicate. The more the animal expresses itself, the more you feel alive. At first your fantasies are like everyone else's. But the deeper your inner animal digs, the further you will go away from the mainstream.

Once you reach a place where your fantasies are individual, you start to see you, the person beyond the preconditioned beliefs and cultural norms.

This often leaves you questioning your life. Why have you chosen a boring career and stable home life? Why do you sit in front of the TV or computer instead of having sex with your hot single neighbor? Why haven't you put the moves on your gardener? Why are you not exploring the depths of your sexuality with your long-term partner?

If you are stuck in rigid patterns, you have to be frustrated enough to change. The power is in freely exploring different sides of yourself without remorse. If you

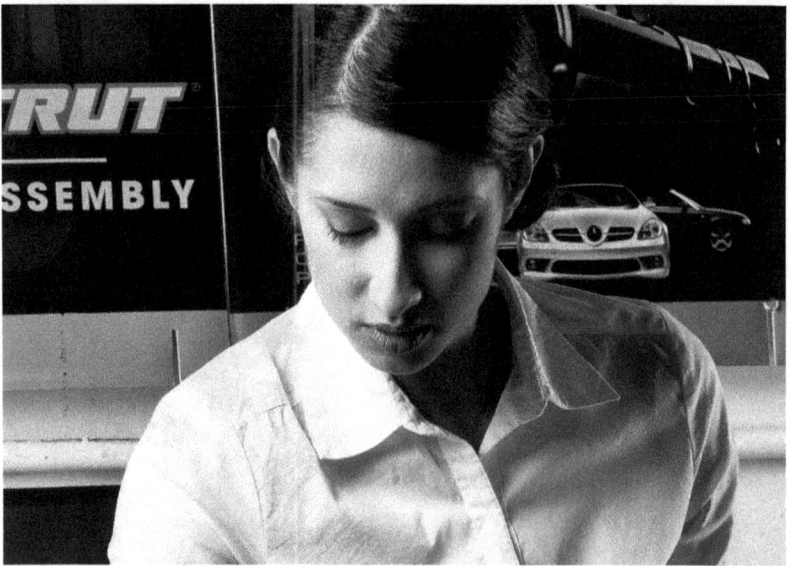

consciously choose to live a boring life, so be it. But if you claim to have full sexual expression, you inevitably have to unravel your desires and dive into your sexual fantasies.

Living out fantasies is a fast way to move through things that prevent you from having a killer sex life. The reason is that it unlocks desires and puts you in touch with parts of yourself that are wild, sexy and unstoppable. Exploring them is the closest you will get to omnipotent pleasure. An article on Askmen.com states that "those who had more sexual fantasies also had higher sexual desire and sexual satisfaction. Pleasure fuels a desire for more pleasure. And while there exists a common false belief that men daydream about sex every seven seconds or so during their waking hours, women also frequently fantasize, especially after they have become aroused."[3]

If you are in a long-term relationship, you have an advantage. There is a level of trust and exploration between you two that has developed over time. You know one another and are more likely to help each

other unveil forbidden desires. Couples with a strong emotional connection have more satisfying sex. A partner who is into you will do everything in his or her power to appease you and fulfill your fantasies. If your partner is not like this, dump 'em. You are deserving of someone better. It is pointless to be with someone who can't accompany you in your sexual liberation.

> "You should become aware that buried in his or her favourite sexual fantasy is a core of desire to experience a special psychological attitude or activity and the accompanying physical sensations. You won't really know your lover until you have unearthed those hidden desires. Nor will you have achieved complete trust and intimacy until you have been able to share your fantasies with each other and have them accepted."[4]
>
> Foreword by "J" in *My Secret Garden* by Nancy Friday

To Nancy Friday, fantasies are not just inner movies that add spice to sex. The function of fantasies is to deal with a frequently unexplored mix of frustration, love and rage.[5] In other words, they facilitate an opening to your core nature or animal inside.

STRANGER

At night in a pitch-black room, your partner can be anyone you want him or her to be, from a person who climbed through your window to have sex with you to a someone you ran into in the hallway. Whatever the scenario is, give it to him/her like you are never going to see them again.

SEX IN PUBLIC

Start getting it on at your favorite beach or park. When random people are walking by, loudly tell your partner what you want to do sexually. The appeal is as much in the shock value as it is in breaking a taboo.

1 2

3

ROLE PLAYING

Ask your partner to play stripper, with you as the patron. Bring reality to the situation by dressing the part. Embody the role like you are a hot Hollywood star with a White Trash attitude.

FORCED SEX

Knock on the door, push it open, gently throw your partner against the wall and give it to him or her. The more your partner succumbs, the more they can enjoy the experience.

4

5 6

BONDAGE

Use soft hand cuffs to tie your partner up and start to give them inescapable sexual pleasure. Bedroom bondage is different from BDSM where there is generally no sexual contact and some infliction of pain.

VOYEURISM

Request that your partner masturbate while you peek through the doorway and watch. Don't start anything sexual until your partner is done pleasing himself or herself.

Power play in fantasies illustrates the same underlying theme: it is a turn-on to dominate and be dominated. Maggie Gyllenhaal as Lee in the movie *Secretary* is dead inside. She is surrounded by dysfunctional people. Just as numb as they are, she doesn't let anything into her world. Neither pain nor pleasure.

Not until she meets James Spader as Mr. Grey, a demanding lawyer who hires her as his assistant. Lee goes from being a meek typist to a sexually awakened secretary. Her liberation comes through living out fantasies with Mr. Grey in the workplace. Her darkness fades through their honest, steaming hot communication.

> MR. GREY (G): DO YOU REALLY WANNA BE MY SECRETARY?
>
> LEE (L): YES, I DO.
>
> G: THIS ISN'T JUST ABOUT TYPOS, TAPES, STAPLES AND PENCILS, IS IT, LEE?
>
> L: NO, SIR.
>
> G: WHAT?
>
> L: NO, SIR![6]

The whole point of this book is to highlight different aspects of liberation so your life, like Lee's, can be taken to higher levels of passion and spontaneity. The deeper you address your fantasies, the more you can feel the real you behind all the social conditioning.

At one stage, your fantasies may fade and pure desires may come without visualization or imagination. Ultimately this is what you want to have happen. You want to be able to feel ecstasy without any enhancers. It is at this point that sex becomes deep and satisfying.

The first episode of *Californication* is the epitome of sin-sational. David Duchovny as Hank goes to church to confess that he is having a crisis of faith because his writing is leading nowhere. A nun steps in and that's when the anointing begins...

"Normally I would suggest a bunch of Our Fathers or a couple Hail Mary's. But I don't think that is going to get it done."
(Long sigh from Hank)
"What about a blow job?"
"Uh?!"
"A blow job. Would that make you feel any better?"
"A blow job from you?"
"Well something tells me it's not going to suck itself Hank."
"No, but. But, you are a nun. A totally fucking hot nun."
(Hank covers Jesus' eyes and says:)
"Sweet baby Jesus. Hank is going to Hell."[7]

SEXCESS/•

High flying bankers on Wall Street, CEOs, A+ students, Olympic champions, billionaires, car mechanics, fast food employees, starving musicians, ex-convicts and everyone in-between, all want more. Nothing is good enough, sometimes not even sex several times a day.

"GREED IS GOOD!"[1] Michael Douglas in *Wall Street*

Success is defined as "the attainment of wealth, position, honors or the like."[2] Society's predefined variables place a burden on people to prove success in a particular way. Peter has a hummer and two girlfriends to display wealth. Sue earns a PhD from a prestigious university to prove her position. Pamela gets fake boobs to be envied by her friends and desired by men.

What do people do to be viewed as successful where you are from? Can they be satisfied without flaunting conventional signs of success? How about you? Do you do things you don't want to because that is

what successful people are supposed to do? Do you follow trends without thinking about whether or not they fit with what you want?

When it is easy to classify a culture "For us Australians, it's very stylish to..." or "We Swedes all like...", hear the alarm bells going off. Such beliefs are not individual but are a cultural creed. They sweep through the masses in the form of norms and values. Even when they are different in their cultural context they have a commonality, which is to steer people away from liberation.

Which norms did you sign up to? A hip city life in a classy apartment with obligatory dining out and dress codes? A suburban lifestyle with an occasional neighborhood BBQ? A remote location with fewer people than trees?

Once you start to see how you fall into the hands of society's stipulations, you can choose to unplug yourself, if you dare.

"

The Matrix is a system, Neo. That system is our enemy. But when you're inside, you look around, what do you see? Businessmen, teachers, lawyers, carpenters. The very minds of the people we are trying to save. But until we do, these people are still a part of that system and that makes them our enemy. You have to understand, most of these people are not ready to be unplugged. And many of them are so inured, so hopelessly dependent on the system, that they will fight to protect it.[3]

Morpheus in *The Matrix*

True success is not what you do or who you are but how you do it. It is dependent on one factor: how you apply your will. When you do something you believe in, not something society tells you is true, and when you are not stopped by anything to get it done, you engage will. *Will* is the ability to achieve things and often ignites in situations of pressure.

You see this in certain movies: A main character, under pressure to survive, suddenly turns from wimp to hero by engaging will. A hidden force comes out and makes him unstoppable. He fights for what he wants, be it love, money or higher truth, and gains the respect of his community. His drive propels success.

Napoleon Hill dedicates a whole chapter to sex and success in his book *Think and Grow Rich*. He states: "sex energy is the creative energy of all genii. There never has been, and never will be a great leader, builder or artist lacking in this driving force of sex."[5]

From a psychological perspective, the driving force for success is stimulated by the same hormones that are triggered during sex. These hormones engender feelings of competitiveness and strength. They fuel an unstoppable fire. People with this element of fire capture others like a Venus flytrap. They are just as predatorial as the carnivorous plant, which makes them successful at getting what they want.

Going for what you want

gets you in touch with

THE SAME ENERGY

that drives you in sex.

They know how to use their body, voice and energy to draw people in. When they sense something they like, they grip their jaws into it. Carrying no remorse for their actions, they thrive off getting what they want. This makes them damn good in bed.

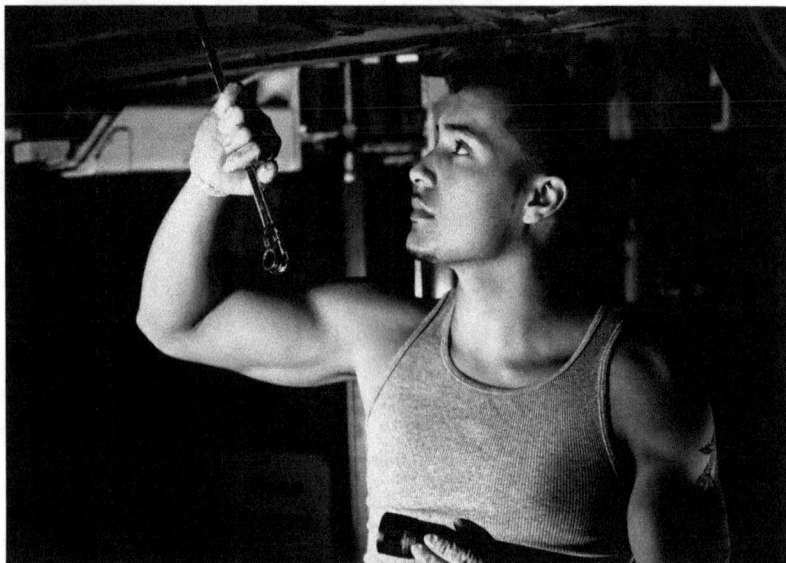

Sexcessful people follow their intuition rather than being caught up in mental chatter and rigid routines. They are able to make spontaneous and intuitive decisions on the fly. By following their gut feelings, they get ahead. Look at Elvis Presley. He is the epitome of someone who followed his desires and paved a path of sexcess.

> **@funnyoneliners** Tampa Bay
> Behind every successful man, there is a surprised woman.[4]
> 2 hours ago

Elvis knew exactly how to use his body, voice and energy to draw women into a frenzy. In 1955, the Florida police forced him to perform without moving. By 1956, Presley was a millionaire. There is no knowing exactly how many women he had during his time but in 1960 when he told his stepmother that he had slept with a thousand women, no one accused him of exaggerating. Between the ages of 20 and 30, he often went through two or three women a day.[6] There is no denying that sex and success go together.

4 Habits of Highly SEXCESSFUL People

ONE SELF-CONFIDENCE

It doesn't matter where you draw it from (money, dick size, new bike or your herb garden behind the kitchen). You just have to be confident about something.

TWO AWARENESS

Have body awareness whether it comes from doing sports, yoga or hiking. You can't be in touch with your body sitting in the office the whole day.

THREE WISDOM

Feel out whether you click with your prospective partner. It doesn't matter if you like or hate them. When you are indifferent, don't waste time. Move on.

FOUR AUTHENTICITY

The first three points save you the need for psycho tricks. Whether you have a one-night stand or long-term relationship, be authentic.

UNCENSORED
CREATIVITY/●

Social norms and creativity go together as well as fat guys and speedos. They don't. Society wants obedience, structure and everyone's pants to be intact while creativity wants spontaneity, anti-establishment and freedom of expression. When creativity confronts society, there is a clash - a sizable storm that has the propensity to damage a whole region. To avoid such disasters, people tend to do what they are told. How can you have sex like White Trash when you follow the norms of society?

"No great genius has ever existed without some touch of madness."
Aristotle

Being great in bed requires an element of uncensored creativity. (Fat guys in speedos may not be so bad after all.)

This creativity comes from a life force inside... That which loves getting down and dirty without stopping to come up for air. That which keeps you creatively engaged and going strong. That which makes you a freak at times. When you live from this force, you tap into the part of yourself that is like a superhero (in speedos if you really push it) and reach the part of you that moves beyond human capabilities, knows pleasure and can ride ecstasy for hours. *Longer, Harder, Better.*

SOCIETY IS AT FAULT BECAUSE IT DOESN'T VALUE THE ABILITY TO FEEL ULTIMATE PLEASURE. RATHER SOCIETY VALUES ALL THE THINGS THAT IT THINKS WILL GET IT ULTIMATE PLEASURE. WHAT ABOUT THE FAT GUY IN SPEEDOS? DOES IT TURN HIM ON? IS HE HAVING THE BEST TIME OF HIS LIFE WHILE THE SEXY GIRL IN THE BIKINI IS WORRYING ABOUT THE TINY BIT OF CELLULITE ON HER THIGHS, NOT ACTUALLY FEELING THE ENJOYMENT OF HOW HOT SHE IS?

When you are uncensored, creativity takes on a new meaning. It is no longer about creating an award-winning piece of art, developing a stellar iPhone app or composing the world's most popular song. Creativity becomes a way of being, which rests on inner strength, confidence and power. It is what makes you unstoppable, turning you into a predator who rides the momentum of pushing ideas through. These ideas don't have to be over the top. They just have to work.

You see uncensored creativity in people who weren't really trying and end up fathoming a genius idea as if the formula fell from the sky. Generally these people can't explain how it happened. Their ingenuity spawned when they weren't thinking. This is creativity.

Creativity is a beyond-the-mind phenomenon which marks the difference between what is real and what is not. It separates the true geniuses from the wannabes. Thomas Edison pushed through more than 10,000 ideas before he came up with the incandescent light bulb. Marie Curie worked in subpar conditions while

developing methods for the separation of radium, which eventually led her to receive the Nobel Prize, twice. Albert Einstein published theory after theory before devising his formula $E=MC^2$.

Where did their ideas flourish? Maybe not in some dark inconspicuous lab. Perhaps their theories fell from the sky while they were having a quickie on the kitchen table. After all, Thomas Edison fathered six children, Curie was in a year-long affair with a former student of her husband's and Einstein had a half a dozen girlfriends.

> "WE MUST ACT."
>
> MARIE CURIE

Sex and creativity go hand in hand. The same life force which is engaged when you are creative is sparked when you have really good sex. There is a flair of vision which takes you out of the ordinary way of thinking into a realm of inspiration. Also, feelings of romantic love can boost levels of dopamine, a neurochemical associated

with creativity, and sexual desire can raise levels of testosterone, known to promote analytical skills.[3]

It comes as no surprise that one of the greatest composers of all time, Johann Sebastian Bach, had twenty children. This does not imply, however, that people who have a lot of sex and children are always creative. Take Jacob Zuma, the President of South Africa, for example. He, too, has twenty offspring but is not necessarily beaming with prolific inspiration. And then there is Jim-Bob Duggar, former Arkansas legislator turned reality TV star. Someone please convince him to close his shop!

Psychologists at the University of Newcastle upon Tyne and the Open University found that professional artists and poets have about twice as many sexual partners as others. The study also showed that the average number of sexual partners increased as creative output went up.[4] The findings suggest that artistic people don't fall as easily for moral, social and ethical dilemmas. Without the constraints of societal norms, there is room for greater knowledge, depth and creativity.

Leonardo da Vinci is a prime example of an artist who broke away from the traditional ways of 15th-century painting and took creativity to new heights. The natural poses and gestures of his painted subjects stood out from the stiff portraiture common in the Middle Ages. By playing with composition and colors, he created art with depth, volume and shape. His techniques blew every other artist out of the water. Da Vinci's use of uncensored creativity made his work superior to that of all others.

"HE WAS LIKE A MAN WHO HAD AWOKEN TOO EARLY IN THE DARK, WHILE THE OTHERS WERE STILL ASLEEP."

Dimitri S. Merezhkovky on Leonardo da Vinci

1901

You don't have to be da Vinci, Bach, Einstein, Curie or Edison to master creativity. You can be a simple person with practical ideas and still be creative. Charles Mingus said it best:

> " Making the simple complicated is commonplace; making the complicated simple, awesomely simple, that's creativity.[5]

Creativity is using Cool Whipped containers as bowls, an old tire as a planter or bean cans as a wind chime. It is how you engage your talents to make life interesting and fun. The same force you pour into creativity is what can make your sex life out of this world amazing.

KITCHEN QUICKIE/ •

The counter top. The kitchen table. The stove. The sink. They aren't at optimal penetration height (OPH) for nothing. Perfectly positioned for your pleasure, your appliances wait for you to figure out how to use them properly. Some die before you catch on. But most sit patiently anticipating the day when your butt rams against them in hot, passionate sex. They want to support you in your deepest animalistic desires. Those that are centered around food and sex.

> **(614):**
> How to cook rice:
> 1. Put random amount of rice and water in a pot.
> 2. Have sex on the kitchen floor. When you are done having sex the rice is ready.[1]
>
> TextsFromLastNight

The kitchen is the ultimate place to satisfy these two desires. It is the command center and most powerful place in a house. It is the headquarters where ruthless meetings are held and wheelers and dealers are fed. It is the place for heating and spicing things up.

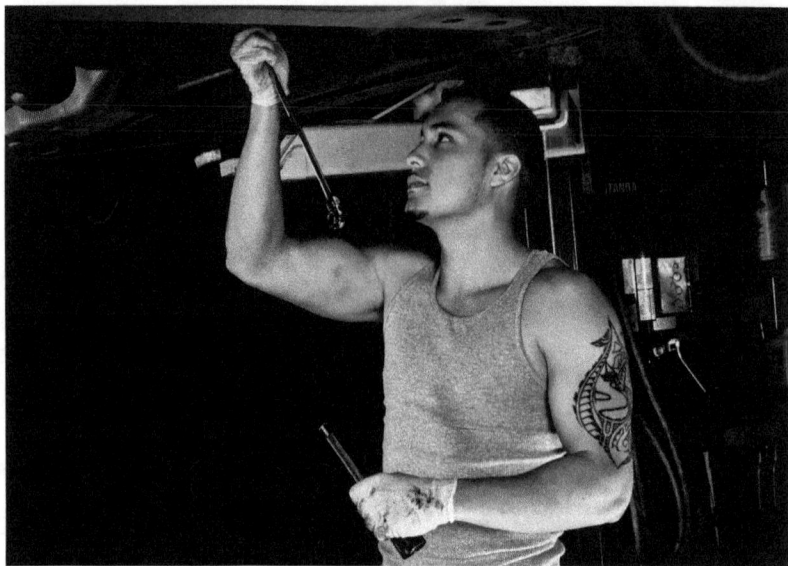

Back in the day, the kitchen was the largest room in a house. It was where people spent the whole day, stirring and melting, making and discovering. Ingredients were mixed and cooked by fire in an alchemical process.

"Tita's emotions and passions are the impetus for expression and action not through the normal means of communication but through the food she prepares. She is therefore able to consummate her love with Pedro through the food she serves. This clearly is much more than communication through food or a mere aphrodisiac; this is a form of sexual transubstantiation whereby the rose petal sauce and the quail have been turned into the body of Tita.[2] *Like Water for Chocolate*

Cooking was and still is a process of living and an activity that provides immense pleasure. It is not just about cutting vegetables. Cooking has a higher component of resonance that can literally transform your sexual relationship.

Once you have cultivated that which brings life to your food, you are on your way to master that which brings life to your sexual experiences. Both use the same ingredient. A passion that comes from within. This passion stimulates senses and brings desires to the surface.

Have you noticed the more you cook, the more you crave sex? And the more sex you have, the more hungry you are? There is a direct correlation between the two, which explains why young adults commonly gain weight when they become sexually active. Cooking and sex both wake something up inside by engaging an intensity in the belly. The more you apply this belly intensity in the kitchen, the better your meals will taste.

29

> Food always tastes better after sex. This we
> ALL know and can count on. Heck, everything
> is better after a damn good lay! We can always
> count on everything being deliciously wonderful
> post good sex. It is the before sex, or the "pre-
> sex" events that really reveal a person's know-
> how in the whole thing. My forte: Cooking.

I love food as much as I love sex. I make love
to my food like I make love to a man. I know it
sounds a bit like cheap romance novel type shit
but I'm being serious. There is no other option!

Every man I have made love to, I have also
cooked some irresistibly yummy food for. It's

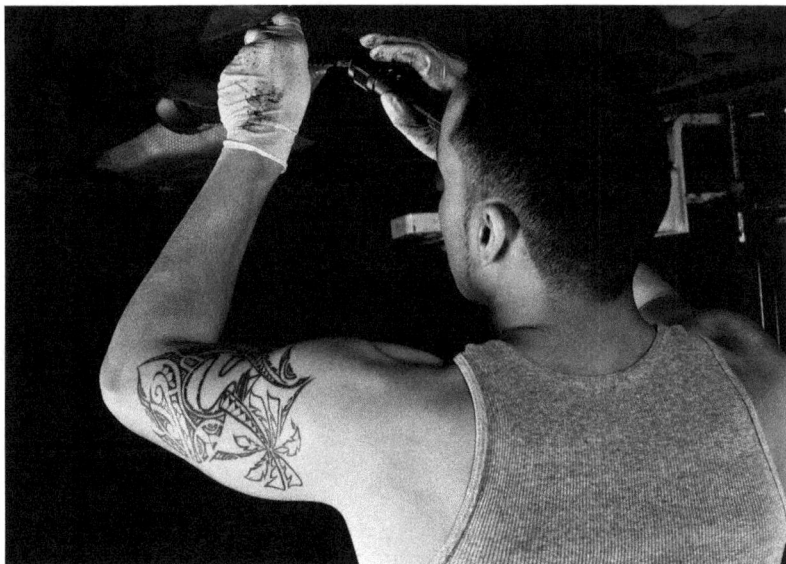

just what needs to happen. My belly has needs. Actually, all bellies have needs! It's just that my belly's needs often are on a different wavelength that rests on feeling myself in a new way. I have finally let go to this, and I now always go with what my belly needs (and wants!) when it comes to Food and Sex. I never hold back. It usually wants very luscious, very yummy, very creamy and very abundant things (food and men alike). It hasn't caused me any harm…yet.

One night, before the man even stepped into my house for an evening of pleasure, fun and some damn good homemade cuisine, I had already begun the process of meeting my belly's needs. Not even thinking specifically about the guy who was going to enjoy my company and my food, but simply gearing myself into the space of my own pleasure, my own fun. I started by putting

on sexy clothes (I told you, I MAKE LOVE to
my food!) and some sexy music.

And so it began. Even before I started to cut the
vegetables and boil the water for the pasta, I was
in it. There was nothing anyone could do to stop
it. He would soon discover the best damn pasta
he had ever tasted. Oh, and the sex was amazing
too!

This is where I tell you, it is worth learning to
cook (even a bit). If you can get a few recipes
under your belt and feel comfortable with
the methods and tools used, then comes the
pleasurable part. The lovemaking part!

Once you tap into the pleasure, that part of your
belly that knows what it wants and needs, every
spice you add, every sauce you stir, is nothing

short of a pure alchemical creation in the making. Everything that happens after that is pure magic! I taste my creations in the kitchen from this pleasurable part of my belly, and adjust seasoning accordingly. A warning, if you should ever decide to tap into this part of yourself in the kitchen: Your sex is going to become greater, it's going to become more pleasurable and it's going to deeply satisfy parts of yourself you never knew existed.

I'm sure you can handle it."

29

San Francisco, CA, U.S.A.

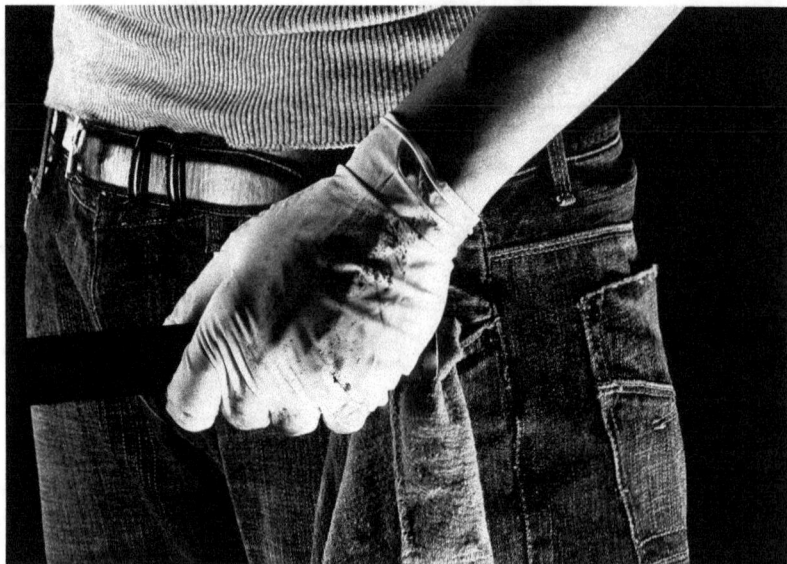

What you do with your energy while you are cooking ultimately ends up in your food. If you are in a bad mood, your food is not going to have the same aliveness as when you are in a playful mood. This is why the same exact meal can be great one time and not the next.

When your belly is jolly rather than uptight, you add a flavor of warmth to the meal. This warmth is passed on to those who eat your food. Cooking is just as intimate as sex in this regard. Especially when you pour pure emotions into your food.

The moment Brittany Murphy as Abby in the movie *Ramen Girl* gets in touch with how she feels, the inner qualities of her ramen change. The people who eat her ramen get in touch with their own feelings. And subsequently, she finds a sexually satisfying relationship.[3]

When you don't pour passion into your cooking, and into your sexual activities, you end up creating something that is dull and lifeless.

[1]

Think of yourself as a temperature gauge. Test the doneness of your meal without opening the oven, or keep tabs of your partner without having to ask how they are. You can see it in their eyes. You can smell it in their expressions. You can taste it in their movements.

these ain't no cookie cutter solutions

[2]

Prepare your favorite recipe without using measuring devices or a timer. Stir in amounts that feel right to you. Don't monitor the time. Simply cook the meal for as long as you feel is right. While your food is cooking, feel what the heat in the kitchen does to your body. Feel the sensual sensations that bubble to the surface. If you do not cook, start by using an easy recipe. Rely on your instincts and feelings as much as on the knowledge of materials and methods.

[3]

Maintain a high level of confidence even when you don't know what you are doing. Fake it until you bake it.

Ultimately, the same spice that goes into cooking can be stirred into sex. The same knowing of when to turn up the heat or when to slow simmer can be applied beneath the sheets. The more you rely on the knowing that you use to cook, the more satisfaction you will bring to your partner when you get it on in bed.

The next time you are finishing up your cereal and getting ready to take off to work, grab your partner for a quickie on the kitchen table or stove. It sets the space for the day and makes you feel great. When you get home at night, have sex before, during and after dinner. Feel the difference it makes to the food and eating experience.

> "Sex in the kitchen over by the stove
> Put you on the counter by the buttered rolls
> Hands on the table, on your tippy toes
> We'll be making love like the restaurant was closed."[4]
>
> R. Kelly

FIGHTING
& FUCKING/ •

ighting and fucking. There is not much difference between the two. The same intensity that gears into fighting is what goes into sex. There is a rush of adrenaline that moves you towards the core of yourself - the animal that wants more. It creates a sensation that gets you high. *Blood pumping. Heart racing. Body moving.*

ighting and fucking. They both make you feel on top of the world. Punches or thrusts, you feel powerful. Moans or groans, you feel victorious. Pain and pleasure, you feel alive. After having a good fight or getting laid really well, everything else is insubstantial.

During a fight or sex, chemicals like adrenaline, noradrenaline and cortisol are released into the body. There is a level of awakening and the senses are completely acute. Nothing tops the feeling of aliveness, invincibility and power.

> "AFTER A NIGHT IN FIGHT CLUB, EVERYTHING
> IN THE REAL WORLD GETS THE VOLUME
> TURNED DOWN. NOTHING CAN PISS YOU
> OFF. YOUR WORD IS LAW, AND IF OTHER
> PEOPLE BREAK THAT LAW OR QUESTION
> YOU, EVEN THAT DOESN'T PISS YOU OFF."[1]

CHUCK PALAHNIUK, *FIGHT CLUB*

It is no surprise that Mike Tyson had at least three girlfriends at the peak of his career. That which led him to crush his opponents, regardless of their size, is what led him to please his women. A man who knows how to get into his intensity is a man who can satisfy a woman. A woman who knows how to hold the intensity is a woman who can keep a man.

This intensity is not physical. It comes from inside. In the Fyodor Productions documentary, Tyson explains that he learned from Cus D'Amato that fighting is spiritual.

> "Without the spiritual warrior in you, you will never be a good fighter no matter how big and strong you are."[3]

Cus D'Amato

Before D'Amato allowed Tyson to step foot in the ring, he taught him the psychology of fighting. "Your mind is not in the way," he would say to Tyson. "There is nothing distracting you." D'Amato was onto something. In fighting and in sex, silence is key. When your mind is silent, you can experience amazing moments of existence.

In stillness, you move into a new dimension that is completely out of this world, beyond the physical. If you push silence in sex, you can ride a wave of ecstasy for hours. This is when sex really becomes a path to liberation.

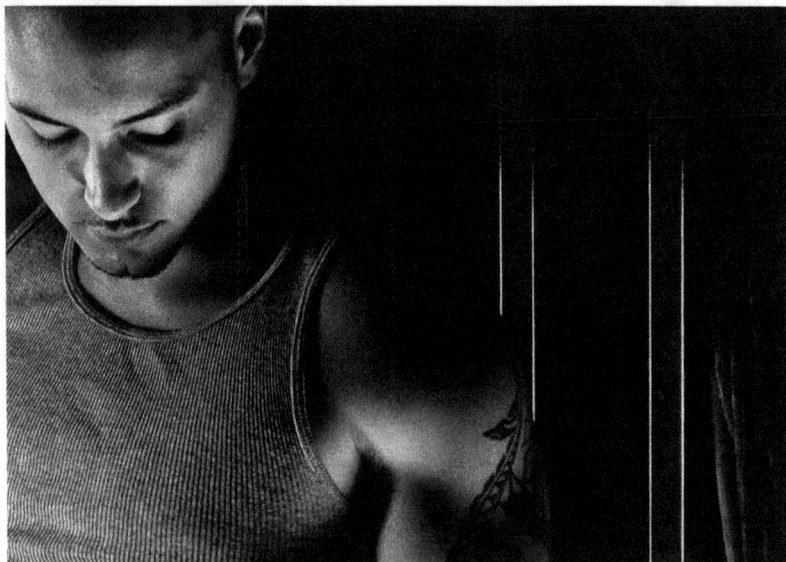

THOUGHTS ARE WHAT KILL YOU. They keep your body clinging onto something that is not real. Your focus is somewhere outside the experience creating a shopping list, planning a business meeting, dreaming about your next vacation or fearing a disaster. You cannot be fully engaged in anything if you are constantly being distracted by meaningless thoughts.

In sex as well as in fighting, a letting go needs to happen. You may experience this as a release of tension in your muscles, a calmness from within or a slowing down of thoughts and worries. It is the same experience runners have when they get into "the zone." In this state, they are at their peak and are focused, self-trusting and relaxed.

If you do not relax in sex, you will not experience full-on pleasure. Now sorry guys but this pleasure is really meant for women. Your kick in the game is to satisfy her. When her look says *Hey what's next?!*, it is time to revise your strategy. When you roll over and see a blissful smile, you know you have done your job.

Sometimes it is unclear which brings more pleasure, sex or fighting. The animalistic part inside can't discern between the two. It just wants to have a kick. It wants intensity and does not care what form it comes in. Once this part has what it wants, it settles down and becomes docile.

The word fuck derives from the Latin root pug, from the verb *pugnare*, which means "to fight."[2]

A classic example is the high-pitched, aggressive woman type who constantly nags her partner for this and that. Altogether it is obvious that she needs to get laid really well and everything would be fine. But without an avenue to let go and access her intensity, she continues to be annoying.

Bitchiness often derives from the same desire that is behind sex, a desire for intensity and resonance with another person. The wars you start with your partner are to satisfy this part of yourself. A strategy the next time a fight breaks out is to turn your aggression towards sexual desires.

Get the charge out of the way by having sex instead of verbally assaulting your partner. Take your feistiness into the bedroom. Demand that your clothes be ripped off and that you be thrown on the bed. Turn your temper into a positive sexual interaction.

Someone who says "I'm a lover not a fighter" is either a peace loving hippie on too much pot, a new-age believer channeling Gandhi, a self-delusional positive thinker or a hypocrite.

Sex works under the principle of balanced opposites. Order does not exist without there first being chaos. There can be no peace without conflict, no light without dark and no pleasure without pain. This polarization creates a means for a broad range of expression.

Your sex life takes on a new dimension when you do not hold back and can freely express whatever it is that you feel, be it violence, passion, excitement, softness, rage or lust.

> ## Cultures that repress sexuality are violent.
>
> James W. Prescott

The type of person who rejects fighting rejects a primordial quality of life. This life force is what fuels the fire in sex. It is what drives the passion for stellar performance. *Longer, Harder, Better.*

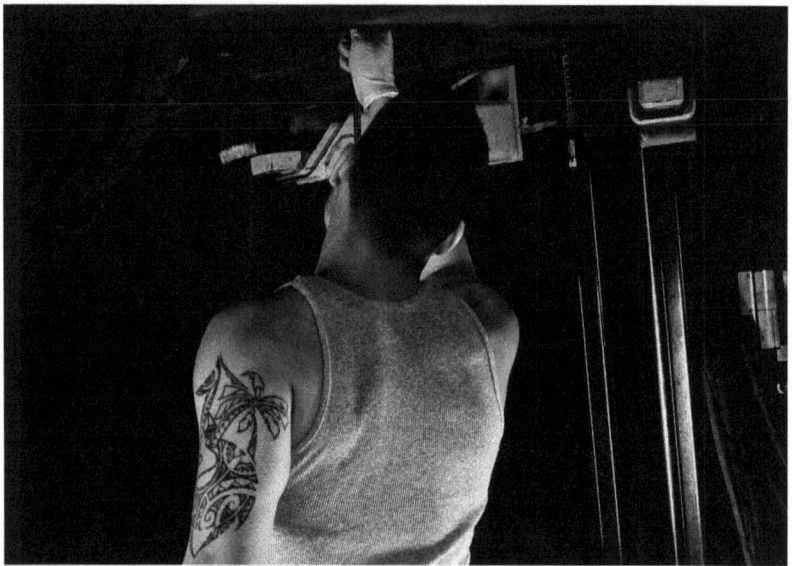

After a gut-wrenching argument, sex is uninhibited. There are no more unspoken words. The pent-up aggression is gone. All cards have been thrown on the table and there isn't anything to feel but a raw essence of life. The sex scene on the stairs in the movie *A History of Violence* is a perfect illustration. It is passionate. It is aggressive. It is real.

Once Viggo Mortensen as Tom Stall is in touch with his violence again, sex is better, his children obey and he becomes Joey, his real self.[4] Being conscious of his violence, ironically, gives him a choice of which side to be on, instead of falling to one side by default.

A History of Violence depicts an aspect of life people need to face: a destructive animal instinct lays deep in the heart of everyone. Whether you are living the lifestyle of the rich and famous or standing in a welfare line, violence is all around. Violence is in you as well as in each person you pass on the street. Those who deny it live locked up in repression as a do-gooder son of a bitch. Those who feel it have sex. Lots of it.

SEX AND VIOLENCE IN THE BRAIN

NEW YORK — Scientists have found a link between sexual arousal and violent behavior.

Aggression in male mice has been tracked to neurons in the brain associated with sex. By loading neurons in the hypothalamus with a light-sensitive protein, Dayu Lin, lead researcher now at New York University, can turn docile mice into fighters.

Lin found there was only one way of preventing violent attacks - sex.

If the males were having sex with a female at the time of the burst of light, it had little effect on their behavior.[6] Once the mice ejaculated, they went back to being provoked by the light. One conclusion is that the act of sex suppresses neurons in the brains that trigger aggression.

The hypothalamus and nearby regions are some of the most ancient parts of the mammalian brain so their functions may not vary greatly between mice and humans.

STAIN THE SHEETS/ •

In White Suburbia, everything needs to stay clean and look perfect - all the time. Beds have become oversized pillow holders, not a place to dive in for a quickie. God forbid a drop of cum might land on the duvet.

On the other side of town is **SEXUAL LIBERATION**. There beyond the tall brick wall is a place where people do not give a shit if the sheets are stained. The bedding can even be ripped and it does not stop them from shaking the bed like a 9.0 earthquake.

Is your bed for sex or for show? Do you have decorative pillows that take over your space or can you jump right in between the sheets when it is time to get down? Great sex happens in optimal places. If your bed is not an optimal sex spot, it is time for change.

Watch how Polly liberates Reuben in the movie *Along Came Polly* (search for the pillow scene on YouTube[1]). Ripping a knife into expensive goose down pillows

can unlock sexual repression. Freud would be the first to say that people's strong instincts toward sex are repressed in order to meet the constraints of a civilized life. In today's society, these constraints are highly materialistic. As the world moves towards consumerism, more and more people are drowning their sexual desires in useless products. Guys are just as guilty as girls. Instead of buying frilly products, they maintain a sizable collection of electronic devices.

FRY'S ELECTRONICS®

The *Victoria's Secret*® FOR MEN

The signs of constraints are showing up in all shapes and sizes. There are more than three stain removers competing for shelf space, for example. Tide® "silences stains instantly," All "goes right to the stain and just lifts it away," OxiClean® "actively breaks down and lifts away stains" and Seventh Generation® is "tough on stains and gentle on the environment." These companies are pushing hard to turn people into a bunch of neurotic wack-jobs.

It doesn't stop at stain removal manufacturers. Each time you go to the grocery store you are bombarded by messages: "Don't smell" "Don't get sick" "Don't grow older" "Don't forget hand sanitizer." Honestly, how much are you going to take from the propaganda of these mobsters before you say *Fuck You, let me live my life!*

You've got to stand up for yourself in this crazy little world. If you follow the norms of society, you'll end up believing shit like hand sanitizer leads you to a healthier life. The only thing you should be concerned about regarding a healthier life is that you are having

amazing sex. It is a really simple solution but commonly overlooked. And the thing is, the more you focus on having White Trash sex, the less impact all of this will have on you.

White Trash sex brings confidence and assurance to the point where you don't have a problem telling people to get fucked. It's hard to buy into propaganda when you are a powerhouse who follows what you feel is right, not what society tells you is right.

The idea is to **LIVE FREE FROM DOGMAS**. When you show up without society's prescribed ways of how to act and be, you relieve yourself from a lot of pressure. This theme is not new. The premise of Jane Austen's 1796 book *Pride and Prejudice* is that relationships work only if a couple escapes the warping effects of society.

Social connections interfere with the courtship between Darcy, the man of pride, and Elizabeth, the queen of prejudice. Only after judgments are dropped can they see through the veil of society and admit their love for

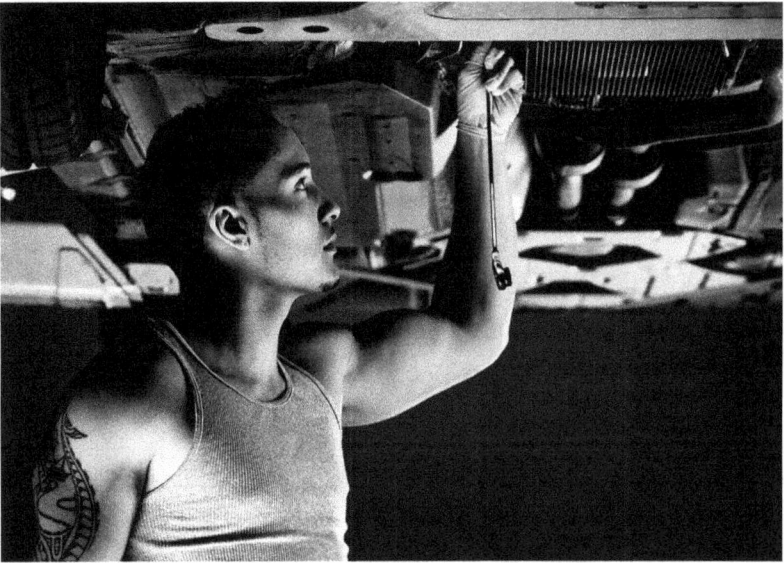

one another.[2] Speaking of her book, check out the Jane Austen version of *Fight Club* on YouTube.[3] It illustrates what would happen if classy Victorian chicks decide they have had enough with the formalities of a polite society. Carried over to sex, it means for you guys that you don't need to uphold the pressure of having to perform well all the time. For you girls, it means that you can drop the pretenses and act totally tasteless. It's liberating to be authentic!

> LIVING FREE FROM DOGMAS BEGINS BY CLAIMING OWNERSHIP OVER WHAT IS YOURS. WHEN YOU DON'T MARK YOUR TERRITORY, YOU ARE NOT IN CHARGE. BEGIN BY STAINING YOUR SHEETS. BE LIKE A WILD ANIMAL BUT INSTEAD OF SPRAYING URINE EVERYWHERE TO COMMUNICATE OWNERSHIP, SPREAD YOUR SEED. LEAVE A MARK OF CUM AS A PROPERTY DEED TO STAKE YOUR CLAIM.
> *THIS IS MY BED AND I'M CLAIMING IT!*

Claiming your bedroom as a hot sex spot requires that you do up your bedroom the way you like. The more comfortable you are in your bedroom, the more fun you will have in it. If there are things you don't like

in your bedroom, get rid of them. This includes unused items in your closet, memorials from your exes, gifts from people who have no taste or junk you have inherited. Your bedroom is a love shack. It is a full service station. It is a place where you can freely express yourself. Do it up accordingly.

Love Shack,
that's where it's at!
Huggin' and a kissin',
dancin' and a lovin',
wearing close to nothing
cause it's hot as an oven.
The whole shack shimmies![4]

B-52s

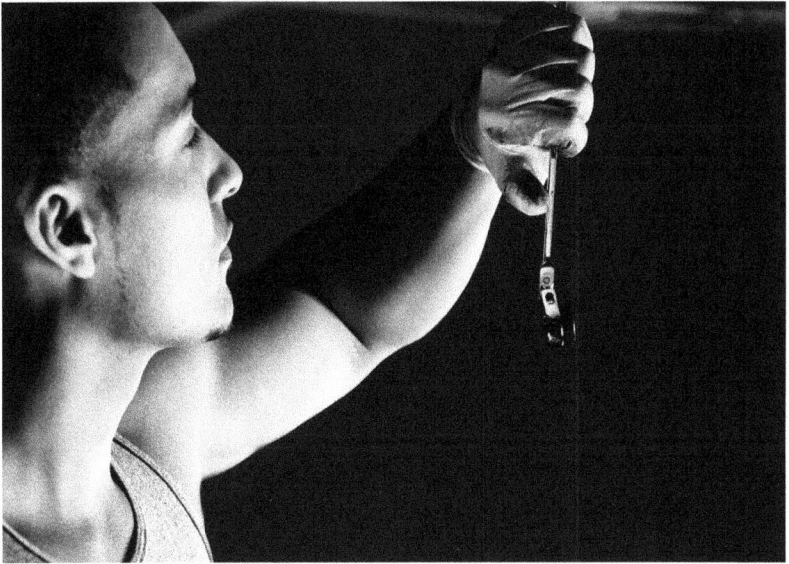

YOU CAN'T "OWN" A PLACE
AND MARK THE TERRITORY IF
YOU DON'T DO ANYTHING TO IT.

PUT YOUR ENERGY INTO IT.

PAINT THE WALLS.

FIX WHAT IS BROKEN.

BUILD YOUR OWN FURNITURE.

ASK YOUR PARTNER WHAT HE OR
SHE NEEDS - A SHELF, A TABLE
OR A SEPARATING WALL. GET THE
MATERIALS AND GO TO WORK.

RAM YOUR STAMP INTO THE CREATION.

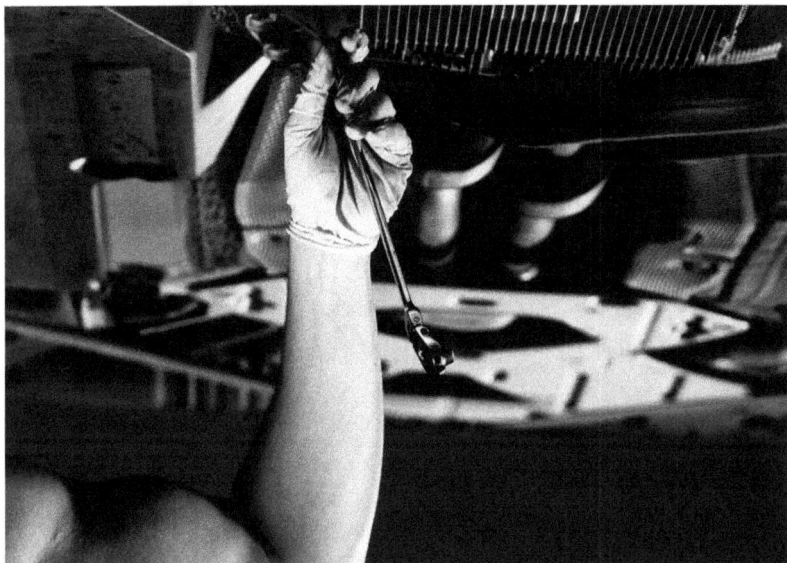

SMELL LIKE A MAN/ •

Smelly French, this chapter is for you. Although the toxic fumes of your armpits are putting holes in the ozone layer, you don't cover up what is you. You prefer everything au naturel. For this, you have a right to be arrogant. You smell like a man and are proud of it, as you should be. Hiding what is natural goes against human nature. It denies that simple things in life bring mind-blowing pleasure. *Joie de vivre*.

The raunchy smell of sweat

The chemicals secreted in sweat, called pheromones, release neurotransmitters that directly modify the behavior of the opposite sex. Studies have shown that a man's pheromones can brighten a woman's mood, reduce tension and increase relaxation, all affecting her inclination to have sex.[1] Other studies have shown that when the underarm sweat of women on different menstrual cycles is placed under the noses of female subjects, the cycle of each subject shifts.[2] You have seen this synchronicity happen in females who live in close quarters. Over time, their menstrual cycles begin to align. As if it weren't bad enough living with one bitch on PMS!

arouses desire and enhances sexual performance. It acts as an aphrodisiac. Some companies market pheromone products to "harness the forces of attraction."[3]

Pheromones are well documented in the animal kingdom as the force that controls social behavior, mating and defense. Human behavior, like that of an animal, is heavily influenced by natural scents.

"Follow your nose, it always knows."

Tucan Sam

Getting in touch with smells opens a new world of sexual exploration. Mussolini was said to have liked his lovers to smell a lot. He allegedly enjoyed the smell of sweat. It definitely brings a certain tingling of excitement.

See for yourself. Smell your partner's hair. Smell their body. Smell their underwear. Smell anything your nose leads you to. Appreciating smells is something small that can have a big impact on your sex life.

This includes your own smell. How is it after a long day in the sun? If you are grossed out, ease your way into enjoyment. The more you like your own smell, the more you accept yourself. To be a great sex partner, you have to like yourself in the natural form.

Think back to what it was like one hundred years ago. It was a time when people spent their days tilling, milling and chilling. Working on the land gave them peace of mind. People were connected to nature and didn't have the propensity to run after a synthetic lifestyle because there wasn't one. They ate food from their farms,

used water from their rivers and worked with materials from their land. They made babies, fed babies and housed babies. There weren't a million choices or directions to take. Their lives were simple. The challenge today is to step back into such an uncomplicated lifestyle and go back to being "au naturel."

FLYING SOLO/ •

A guilty pleasure. One that gives you the same sensation as eating from a box of chocolates you know you weren't allowed to have. There's excitement, bliss and satisfaction. When you are there, the line between devotion and instant gratification becomes blurry. It has you going until the last drop. It's sensational. Yet, if you get caught in the act, shame kicks in. *I can't believe they walked in on me. I shouldn't be doing this!* Embarrassment takes over. *What are they going to think of me now?* Mortification pummels any dwindling feelings of indulgence. *I'd be better off dead!* Masturbation is a normal activity that society has twisted to become the meth of sex.

People who masturbate have no self-discipline. They will go blind. They are going to be sent straight to hell. Who still believes this shit? The mere act of releasing tension yourself is

> " Don't knock masturbation. It's sex with someone I love. "
>
> Woody Allen

as harmless as a Jairo jumping bean. Moral or not, everyone does it. When you want to make a point that you can do something by yourself, you masturbate. When you want to get to sleep, you masturbate. When you want to know who is really the boss, you masturbate. There is nothing wrong with it. It's better you screw yourself than have someone else screw you.

As a strategy to reduce teenage pregnancies, the National Health Service of Britain created a pamphlet to encourage teenagers to masturbate instead of engaging in sex with a partner. "Generally speaking, I see nothing inappropriate in suggesting that masturbation is both pleasurable and healthy for both young adults and older adults," New York City-based psychologist and author Joy Davidson said in response to the pamphlet.[2]

However, masturbation is not a long-term strategy. Too much of it, especially in adulthood, indicates that a sexual desire is not being satisfied. Identifying the why behind sexual dissatisfaction can uncover the how for overcoming it. If you are alone, it is time to figure out what is stopping you from finding a partner. If you have a partner, it is

time for the two of you to have a talk about your sex life.

Professor Simon Crowe, head of neuropsychology at La Trobe University, states "The physiology of sex is very complicated and one we know surprisingly little about given how much it affects our behavior. But the different stress responses between penetrative sex and masturbation suggests the biology of one person affects another."[3] A rocking sex life does not exist without an exchange of passion and heat.

These two things don't exist when there is no one to collide against. There must be thermal contact, like in physics where two molecules have to bump into one another to create friction and heat. Masturbating lacks energy transfer from one body to another and thus lacks the primary component leading to sexual satisfaction.

Look at adults who have not had a partner in years. They are often pale. Their eyes don't sparkle. And they have a hard time expressing themselves. Even if they masturbate a lot, it does not meet their need for resonance.

> MASTURBATING IS LIKE DRINKING FROM
> AN EMPTY GLASS. IT DOES NOT QUENCH
> THIRST. OVER TIME IT MOVES FROM BEING
> A WAY TO LEARN ABOUT WHAT FEELS GOOD
> TO A MIND GAME OF DISSATISFACTION AND
> DISAPPOINTMENT.

Once they find a partner, something is sparked back to life. They walk with confidence. They talk with assurance. And, they become more sexually attractive.

There is no substitute for sex. Nothing can replace the thrill of two sweaty bodies rubbing against one another. Nor does anything compare to holding your partner in rapturous devotion.

The reciprocity of passion, love and intensity is extraordinary in a healthy, loving sexual relationship. You are no longer just a drop in the ocean. You are merged and have a sense of purpose. Two is greater than one.

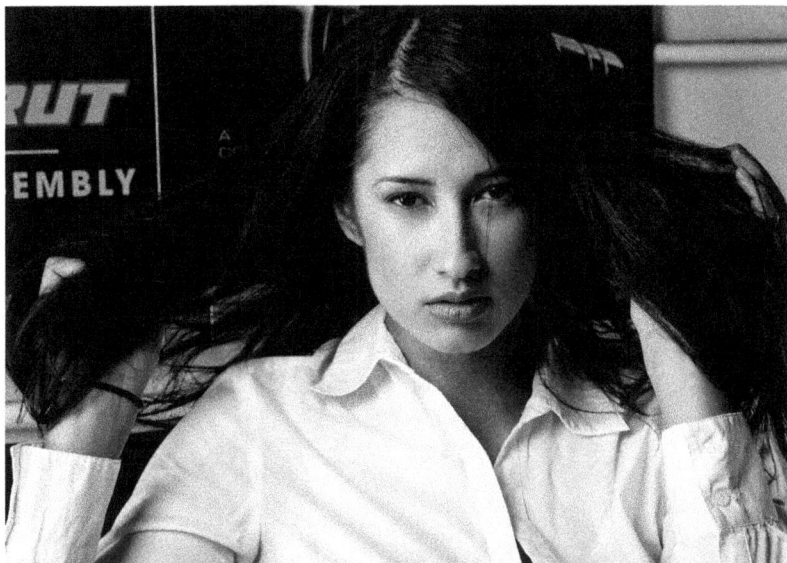

HUNTING FOR
A KEEPER/ •

When you are out on
the prowl for a partner,
it's time to apply your
hunter instincts. It's when
you go in for the kill regardless of size, shape and breed.
For girls this means to hunt guys your dad doesn't
approve of. This type of guy is always great in bed. For
guys this means finding a random pussy to stick your dick
in.

Guys and girls, you should never waste your time on a
person you don't click with. There are so many other
people out there. But before bailing out, make sure it's
that you truly don't like them and not that your societal
beliefs don't fit with theirs. The latter is completely
overlooked by people. It is the reason why some
individuals unnecessarily break up and why others are
never successful in the dating and marriage scene. What
the animal inside likes and what your belief system

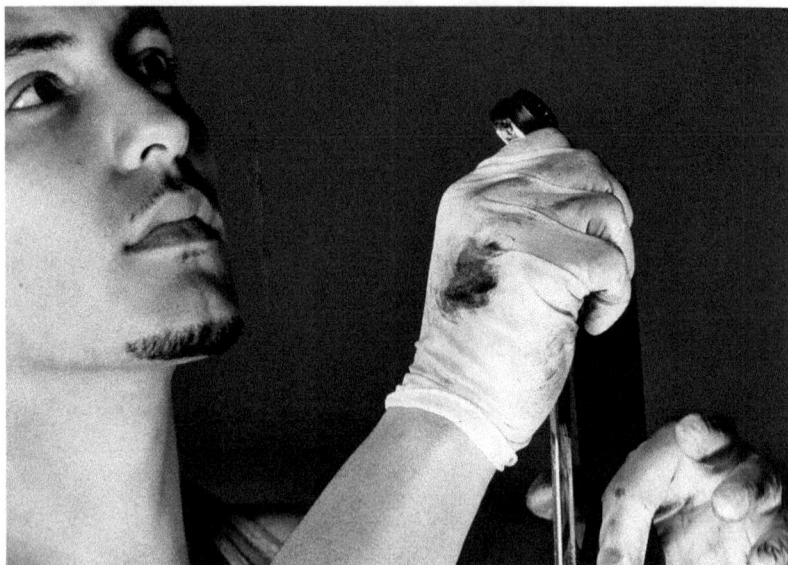

tells you that you like are hardly ever the same. The latter ends up completely boring the former.

You go out with a guy who has it all together. Your family and friends love him. He is smart, financially stable and takes you on romantic vacations. He opens your door, pulls out your chair and walks your dog. He has everything you have ever dreamed of but something doesn't work. He bores the shit out of the part that screams for excitement. You become comfortable with his professional mannerisms but really want to know what he would be like if his White Trash tendencies actually showed.

You are hanging with a girl. She has the body of a goddess. Nice boobs, hips and butt. No need for her to see a plastic surgeon in this lifetime. She's hot and uses it to her advantage. You wonder if that is why she is such a whiney, demanding little thing who is really hard to please. The more you spend time with her, the more you want to see her break out of being a princess into something more slutty. What would she be like if she

showed up in six inch heels, a short skirt and low-cut shirt ready to rock?

When you are on the hunt, consider what your belly wants. In other words, listen to your gut instinct. You might be surprised where you end up and who you shag. And it could be damn worth it! James Huneker put it well when he said:

❝ HE DARES TO BE A FOOL, AND THAT IS THE FIRST STEP IN THE DIRECTION OF WISDOM.

Holding on tight to your pride and prejudices is going to get you nowhere. To find the meat that your belly craves, you have to be daring and do what you want. This may mean shooting pool with rough Harley dudes, frequenting gay bars or hanging out in trailer parks. So be it.

You are doing what your belly wants and are going to feel liberated as a result. A little voice inside might tell you that you are a sinner. It might be mortified by

your behavior. It might even damn you to hell. But you will no longer be pussy-whipped by societal norms. And that feels good! Suddenly you have the balls to get what you want. There is no need to post a partner wanted ad on an online dating site and buy into an industry that rides off people's emotions for money. Car mechanics, cafes, grocery stores, sporting events and bars become good hunting grounds.

Do you ever see White Trash paying for an online dating service? Hell no. Not when there is plenty of hot meat walking the streets.

> **(203):**
> I asked a girl to buy her a drink. She said "I have a boyfriend." So I said "Well I have a goldfish." She said "What?" I replied, "Oh I'm sorry. I thought we were talking about shit that doesn't matter."[1]

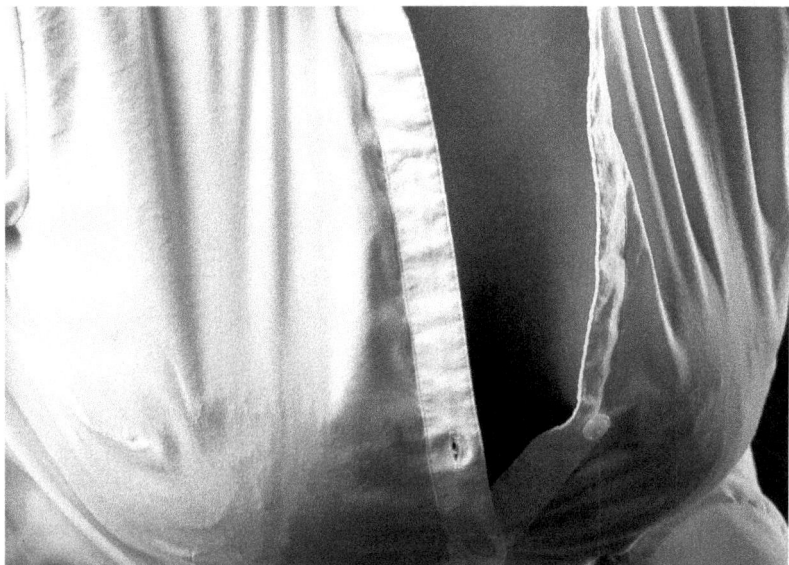

NEED IDEAS?

x Join a group of people who are
  interested in the same things as you.

x Pick up a new sport.

x Move to a more happening place.

x Get a gym membership.

x Hang out at a new club.

x Attend a two-day workshop.

x If all else fails, get a dog.
  They are great people magnets.

OVERSTIMULATION/ •

The music is on, the lights are dimmed and you are both getting hot.

You take off one piece of clothing.

Your partner follows.

You take off another article of clothing.

Then your partner.

You are both playing it slow.

Or so you thought.

The next thing you know, you are out of bed responding to a text message. The person on the other end says it cannot wait. What was going to be a good fuck became a solemn sacrifice to an electronic device.

These things are your pimps. And you are such a good little whore.

Life is becoming more and more fueled with things to distract you. Let's face it, you are addicted to emails, surfing the net and chatting. You may even be hooked on gaming, blogging, talking on the phone or watching television.

PC Tools, a computer security firm, released a study stating that nearly a quarter of U.S. residents think it is fine to be "plugged in" to the internet during sex. The survey, conducted by Harris Interactive, also showed that 29 percent of people in the country believe it is not a problem to be connected online during a wedding and the percentage climbed to 41 percent for family dinners.[1]

There are a million things to pull you away from spending a day rocking and rolling in bed. These things are your pimps. And you are such a good little whore.

As a good little whore, you have a hard time saying no. So instead of doing what you want, you spend hours on things that don't turn you on. You put everything ahead of your own desires. You get pushed around and act out of obligation. Surely this can't make you happy!

With the speeding up of electronics, medicine, consumer products and the like comes a numbing of the senses. This should concern you because it affects your sex life.

When you are constantly being bombarded with emails, text messages, phone calls, blinking internet ads, blaring TVs and traffic, you naturally start to turn the volume down to protect yourself. You make yourself desensitized to outside stimuli. Your sensation of touch gets more dull each time you take the subway home. Your hearing becomes less acute when you drown yourself in loud music. Your sense of smell loses its refinement when you inhale air fresheners, scented candles and other synthetic smells. It's your body's way of coping with the constant bombardment of people and things.

If you take medication or drugs, there is a greater level of numbness. Birth control pills, antidepressants, sleeping pills, cold medicine, alcohol and recreational drugs decrease the capability of sensory organs, increase the rate of cellular deterioration and lower sex drive. Sure, medication reduces pain but at the same time it blocks you from feeling pleasure.

When you are beneath the sheets, you don't want this numbness. The level of satisfaction is ultimately greater when you can feel what is going on inside.

INSTEAD OF REACHING FOR THE ASPIRIN BOTTLE TO GET RID OF YOUR HEADACHE, GO AND GET LAID. SPARK THE ENDORPHINS THAT NATURALLY HEAL YOUR BODY FROM PAIN AND SUFFERING.

During sex, you want the volume turned up. You want to feel everything from the pleasure of your partner to the tingling sensations in your genitals. You want to be taken to endorphin heaven.

If you can't stand to feel pain, you are never going to

push yourself to feel ultimate pleasure. You lack the spark that has the propensity to propel you to go all the way. If you choose to live in mediocrity, so be it. But if you want to cross over to the other side, you are going to have to step into a White Trash roughness. Being in this part is easy to recognize. It likes blood and guts, is not overly analytical and accepts when life is miserable.

Al Bundy: "It's not that I couldn't be happy without you, Peg. It's just that I couldn't be happy. Perhaps that is the true Bundy Legacy."

Peggy Bundy: "I thought the true Bundy Legacy was underwear with just an elastic band."[2]

The trick is to get back in touch with your body through spending time in nature, doing physical work, meditating, going to yoga classes and living in a home with natural materials. These things will help you find your signal in all the noise.

PULLS OF NATURE/ •

You are an upright walking animal, purely primitive in nature. If this primate part had a voice it would say your main purpose for being on earth is to procreate. It wants to populate the world with babies, babies and more babies. It is always there lurking in the background. It fuels your fantasies. It drives your curiosity. It steers your sex drive. When you have sex, your body cries...

"Ten Thousand Babies!!!"

It does not care if your logical mind has decided not to have kids. It just wants to reproduce and pump them out like rabbits.

The urge to procreate can be fierce. When it has a hold on you, sex is nothing more than a few *ews* and *ahs* before the guy spews and the fun is over. If you have any interest in being wild and crazy in bed, whether you are a guy or a girl, you are going to have to acknowledge

these biological desires. For guys, this means you are fighting the urge to ejaculate when all your body wants is for one sperm to find its way to the light. Ejaculation is counterproductive to having sex like White Trash. It cuts into the length of time the session lasts, the pleasure you can give and your level of stamina.

For women, the pulls of nature mean your body is crying to be a mother. Unconsciously or consciously, you want to grow the seed of life inside your belly. Your childbearing hips aren't satisfied with one, two or three kids. They want a whole football team. The pulls of nature are the reason it only takes one night for you to fall completely head over heels, or in your case heels over head, for a guy. Your motherly hormones kick in and steer you straight on. They do not stop to calculate that you have only rolled around with him once. Not when the pedal is full throttle to the metal. *You accelerate.* You can't stop thinking of him. *You obsess.* You declare your love for him. *You dream.* You want him to be the father of your children. *You plan.* You search the web for a house with a playroom for the

kids, a study for him and a big bathroom for you. These pulls of nature work against you in sex because the baby-making mechanics in your body energetically grip onto your guy and can affect how long he lasts.

The more you, man or woman, are aware of nature's pulls and the energetic grips that come along with them, the better you can manage your energy. The pulls of nature can be identified as a tightening in the muscles around the stomach, genitals or perineum. They may cause tension or discomfort. And, they are easily induced by overstimulation. When these subtleties are not recognized, there is a greater chance that a guy will come before he realizes what has happened. End of story.

There are a couple of things that counteract these pulls and let you keep the headboard banging all night long. The first is non-ejaculation. The second is whole body orgasms. This chapter offers an indication of these two topics. Without a doubt, these topics are not for everyone. Also, there is no denying that they are huge.

If you are drawn to learn more, do research, find a system and practice the techniques. See what works for you. It is going to take effort and body awareness. And you will have different results with different partners.

Non-ejaculation

Men, your biological body uses you to procreate. It doesn't care about anything else. When it is in control, it's like a wild horse. You are going to get thrown off into a pool of your semen until you take control of it. Once your horse is tame, a woman can ride it for hours. This is one reason why non-ejaculation is so important. Your purpose in sex is to give a woman pleasure. There is nothing else sex is meant for once the pulls of nature are taken out of the equation.

Having intercourse but not ejaculating may seem counterintuitive. But when a couple is not planning to have a child, it can serve to heighten experiences in both the man and the woman. Dr. Stephen Chang, author of

The Tao of Sexology, questions why an orgasm is called "coming." He sees it more as an act of going.[1] After the excitement builds and the heat is on, there is a sense of coming, coming, coming. Then the load busts and it turns to going, going, going...gone. If the woman is not part of this coming, coming, coming, she is left frustrated.

If you are a woman, you can minimize or counteract this "going" by feeling nature's pulls in yourself. These pulls essentially work to get your man to come. As previously mentioned, you might recognize the pulls as a tightening in your muscles around the stomach, genitals and/or perineum. When you feel your body start to become overly excited, call a time-out.

Women, you are just as responsible for seeing to it that your man does not come as he is. Drawing your attention to other areas besides your genitals helps spread your awareness and feelings of sensuality so the pulls are not as great. The idea of spreading will be explained in the next section.

The more you, the man, practice non-ejaculation, the better you will feel and the longer you will last. Men who have spilled one too many loads look worn out. Taoists say men should avoid ejaculation in order to preserve life essence, or jing. In simple terms what they mean is that you are going to look and feel like shit if you continue to ejaculate day after day. That is why male athletes are told not to cum before a big event. Ejaculation hurts performance and drains youthfulness. Sex is meant to be energizing, not exhausting.

Whole body orgasms

During sex, awareness is generally focused on the genitals. Having a whole body, or full body, orgasm involves spreading your awareness throughout your entire body. Instead of solely focusing on the sensations in your genitals while having sex, start to notice pleasure in your hands, arms, chest, legs and feet. A few things happen when you spread your awareness throughout your body. First, there is a letting go. Second, as you

relax you can access longer-lasting states of pleasure. Third, you take control over nature's pulls.

When you focus solely on your genitals, you keep a tight lock on what happens down there. You grasp onto little sensations in a small area instead of opening to big sensations in a large area. Tension builds up quickly when you are focused on one thing. As explained by one blogger, "By paying attention only to genital sensation, we develop a pattern of 'balloon sex.' We squeeze all of our sensation and focus into a small part of our body, blowing it up until it pops."[2] Releasing your awareness from a single focus can take the edge off. Instead of popping the balloon, you can float in lasting pleasure.

Awareness of more than just genital stimulation takes sex to another level. It strengthens your core and deepens your experiences. With whole body orgasms, you aren't riding on the surface. Such orgasms take you deep and with this comes a feeling of being alive. When you are feeling great, it is easier to get what you want.

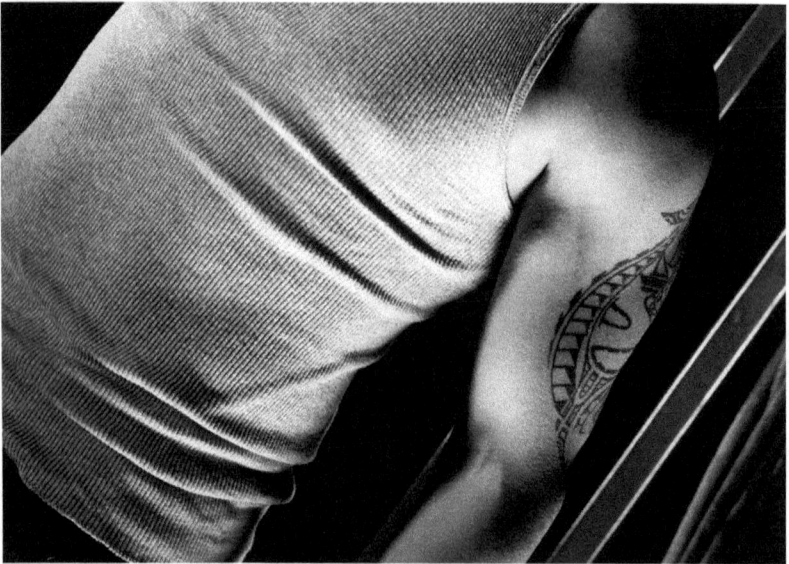

Taking sex from the standpoint of ultimate pleasure, it makes sense to move from wham-bam experiences to long-lasting, full body orgasms. Those that continue through the ninth inning. The more you can allow yourself to experience a whole body orgasm, the better sex you will have. From a little something-something to the whole shebang, whole body orgasms are far more satisfying than nature's pulls for instant gratification.

For some people whole body orgasms happen naturally. For others, it takes a lot of effort and training to experience this different modality of pleasure.

TIPS FOR ACHIEVING A FULL BODY ORGASM

Think global.

Start by taking your focus away from genital stimulation.

Feel different body parts like your hands, legs and feet.

Ask your partner to touch different areas of your body, not only your genitals.

Become aware of the tingling, vibration, pulsing and warmth you feel.

See what happens when you let go into the tingling, vibration, etc.

Connect the sensations to different body parts to reach an all-around orgasm.

Allow the sensations to spread into every cell of your body.

Melt in the pleasure and get ready for more.

MALES ONLY

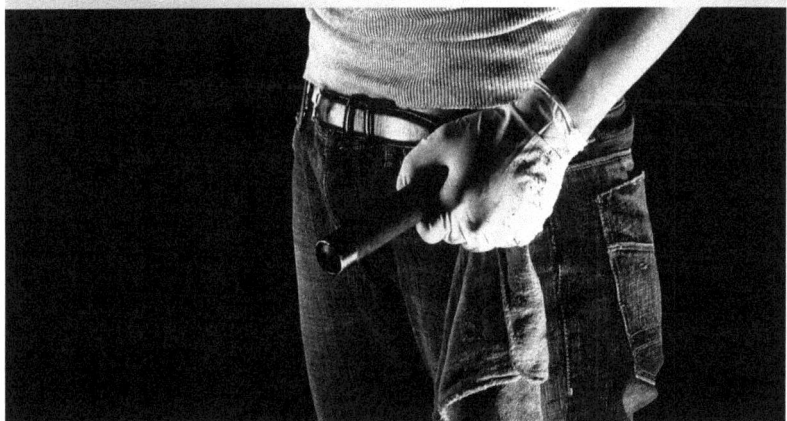

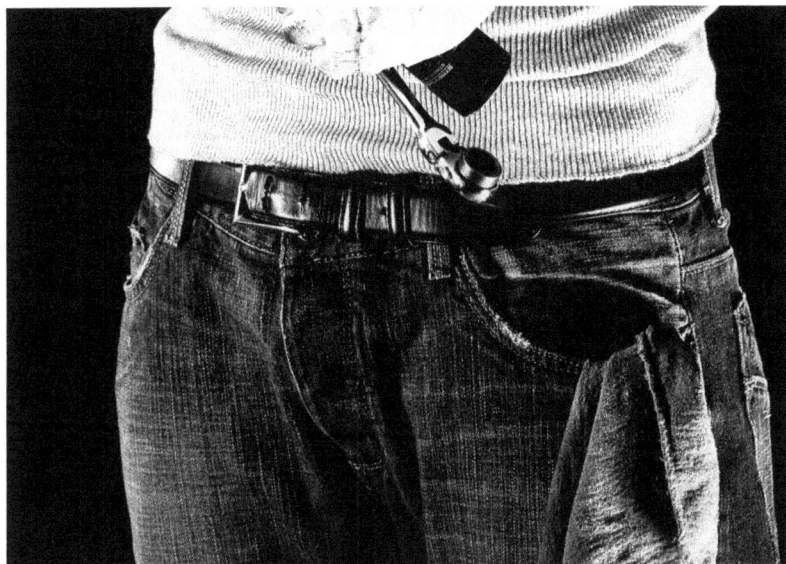

CHICK WITH A DICK/ ■

There are guys who have potential but blow it every damn time. They go home alone night after night without being between the legs of a hot chick. The ingredients are there but they have not mastered the recipe. They simply have not tapped into the part of themselves that is animalistic in nature. *Girls want tiger.* The more the guy has the attitude of getting what he wants, the more attractive he is. *Girls want confidence.* A guy who stands on his own two feet can go down on a woman like a rock star. *Girls want 120 licks per minute.*

From a female's perspective, what's the point in being with a man who isn't good in bed? A guy who can't satisfy his woman should be shot. What a useless tool in a world of hunters! If you are one of these men who just can't get it happening, you are probably nice. You hold deep conversations. You think of others before yourself. You never say anything that is politically incorrect. You behave like a well-trained dog. Moms like you.

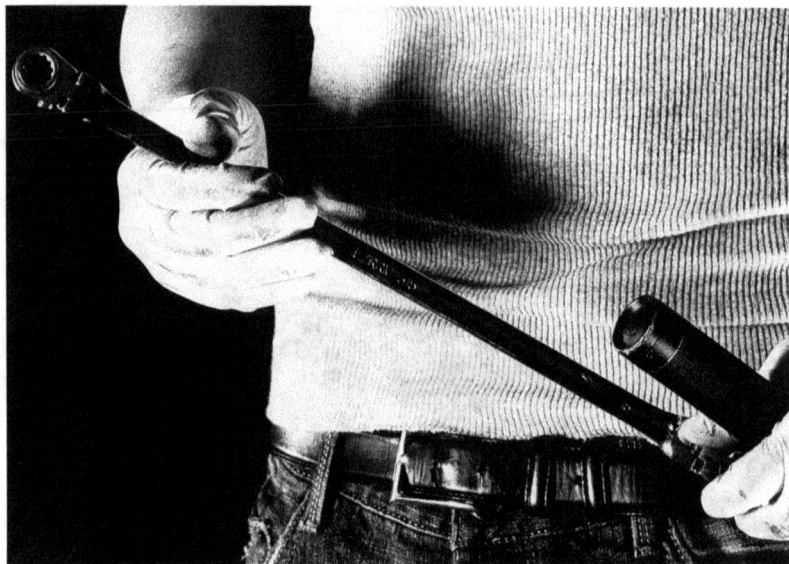

You are the one who has heard more than once from a girl "you are such a great friend." Ouch. Once you have been told "I really like you as a friend but...", forget about it. Put your tail between your legs because you have just been labeled a chick with a dick.

This label is really hard to get rid of. Any chance you thought you had with the girl is gone. Done. You are scratched off her list of potential mates. Now would be the time to move on. And when you do, get a new approach.

What is your favorite animal? Yes, you heard right. Do you prefer cute little kittens over roaring lions? If you do, why? Come on. You are a guy. Testosterone is pumping through you making you more aggressive than a hundred cougars in heat. Dear cuddly kitten, what are you doing with your aggression? Is it locked up somewhere deep inside and no longer accessible? Or is it on the surface but has not had a chance to come out?

What do you do with the part of yourself that can rip a

girl into pieces like a lion on its prey? You know you have it in you. What does this part want from a girl right now? To touch her hard tits? To finger her? To bang her on the kitchen table? Don't stop at these suggestions. Get into the part that can't get enough. You know, the part that eye-fucks every chick who crosses your path.

> **❝** Dustin had a **natural charm** and **animal instinct** that I just didn't. Or at least that's what I thought.
>
> Neil Strauss

Neil Strauss went from being the type who sits alone petting cute little kittens to one who now wrestles with lions. His level of frustration was so great that he found a way out of rejectionland into seductionville. His determination to become a chick magnet led him to an underground community of pickup artists where he learned techniques that worked for him. Strauss now gets what he wants and is known as one of the most successful

pickup artists. "I had clearly become one. When I talked to a woman, the room went silent. The guys leaned in close to hear what I was saying, pulling out notebooks to write my words down and commit them to memory."[1]

The shift he made from a pale-skinned, balding guy with wire-framed glasses to a tanned skinhead with Harley-sculpted facial hair was outwardly apparent. His inner landscape also took a 180. Over a period of a couple of years, he started to embrace his White Trash tendencies. He acted tougher, played hard to get and got crass (and more ass). "I learned that the more unavailable you make yourself, the more people would want you. The more you say 'stop touching me' or 'I'm taken' or 'you're just not my type,' the more people would actually chase you."[2] As soon as he ditched the doormat approach, women actually started showing up at his door. This goes to show that utterly boring niceness does not work in the game of sex. If you are one of these cute little kitten guys, it is time to step into nasty. Getting in touch with your animalistic behavior, especially if you are one of those chicks with a dick, makes you a good fuck.

NICE TO NASTY/ ▪

Why is it that people are ashamed to bring out the White Trash part of themselves? Nasty is a turn-on. Call your lady a bitch while banging her hard. Sure, if she is a prude she might shudder the first time she hears it but watch how much she starts to enjoy it.

Shock her. Unexpectedly throw her in an ice-cold shower. Grab a fist full of her hair when you are heating her up and pull on it hard. Bite her face while kissing her passionately. You get the idea. Be spontaneous to create arousal and excitement.

David Deida says: "Among many other qualities, a woman wants the 'killer' in her man. She is turned off if her man is afraid and wants her to kill the cockroach or mouse while he stands on a chair and watches." Deida claims the fashion in today's world is to "suppress both the dark masculine and the dark feminine, so we have a large population of wimpy men and polite women. But

beneath the nice veneer of most women," he says, "lies the wrathful goddess who would chop the head off of every mediocre 'new age' man."[1]

These mediocre nice guys never move into the nasty category because they are always sorry. They are sorry when they are rough. They are sorry when they say something offensive. They are sorry about this and that. Always sorry. Sorry is what they are when they go to bed without having loud bed-squeaking sex. Sorry is what they are when their life passes them by and they realize their niceness has killed every opportunity to have fun.

Without going into too much psycho-babble, from an early age you are taught that acting nice gets you things. Your mom would give you a treat if you were nice to your siblings. Your teachers would give you an "O" in citizenship if you played nicely with your schoolmates. Nice worked really well when you were young. But it does not work well now. So get with the program. The next time you are too nice, listen to the warning bells going off. Beep, beep, beep - nice alert. Must mean I

want something here, you say to yourself. Then ask,

WHAT WOULD A

WHITE TRASH

GUY DO?

He would be rougher, more verbal and manly. Be
that. Start to nibble on her nape. Pull her hair. Kiss
her behind the ear. Whisper how you like her wet little
pussy. Scratch your nails down her back until it stings.
Pin her to the bed telling her that she has been naughty.
When she gets more turned on, bite her.

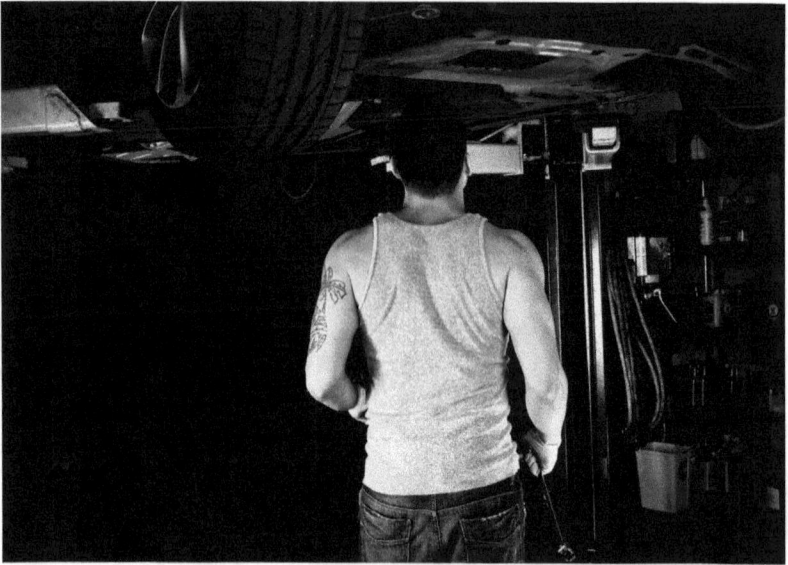

Start slapping her ass in a rhythmic movement. Do not go down just yet. Make her beg for it. Get her hotter. Knead her body. Push her panties to the side. Touch the inside of her leg. Move your head down and start kissing her belly. Let your tongue lead the way. Now gently lick her clit. Move it from side to side. Give her ass a hard squeeze. Start licking faster. Be sloppy. You are getting ready to pin her. Get into your animal. Tell her how she is a whore deserving of a hard fuck. Hear her breathing heavy. She's ready for you to stick your throbbing cock inside. Thrust your hips into hers. Squeeze your hands around her neck. She should be scared of your intensity but not overly so. Back off at times and be soft.

The trick is to know when to be nasty or not. White Trash guys are not assholes. They are simply comfortable in themselves to act on their desires. Let your nastiness come out at the right time and she will beg for more.

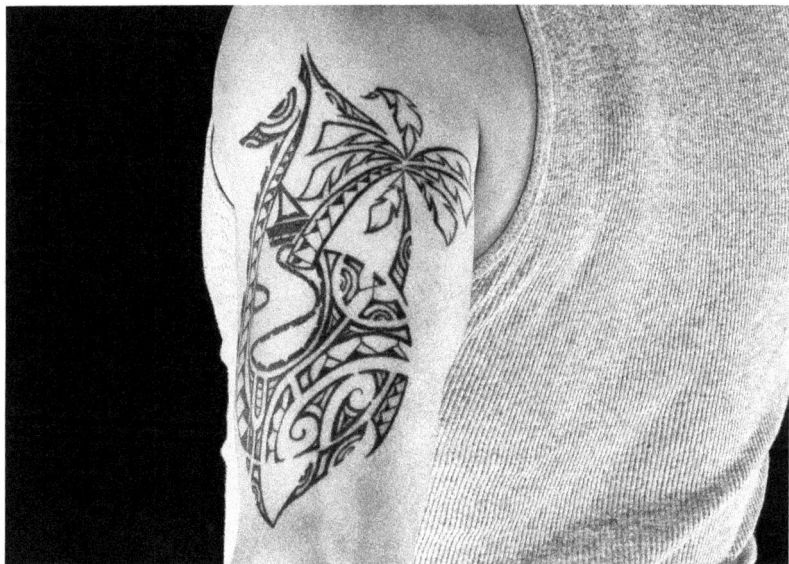

YOU??

YOU?!

MALE **28**

66 It's all about confidence. And even if you can
muster fake confidence, you will get chicks.
Women want a guy who is sure of himself. In
fact, whether most women will admit it or not,
they would rather go out with a dickhead than a
wimp, all things being equal.

Now, if you want to attract a woman who could
be your girlfriend, then being a dickhead is
unsustainable, saved for psychos and strippers.

I recommend you date at least one of those to
get a sense of what you don't want. Besides,
they fuck better. So you can start to ask the

women you do end up liking to do the things the psychos/strippers do.

Nice girls are boring but make a good foundation for a girlfriend. So it is your job as a man to impart a sense of direction and fun into the relationship.

She wants that from you. Ask for what you want and the nice girl will oblige. Within weeks you can go from boring bookworm who gives standard blowjobs to a full-blown slut who will take it up the ass in the mechanics section of the public library.

And she will thank you.

The good news is she won't fuck your friends or steal your money for coke like psycho-sluts will. You just need to listen to her when she goes into

the classic whine and not try to fix anything.

Stay on top. Nod your head. Really listen and don't necessarily offer advice. You stay in control by being a man who knows what he wants, not by controlling her.

Make her feel wanted and she will always give you that handjob in the WalMart parking lot."

28 New York, NY, U.S.A.

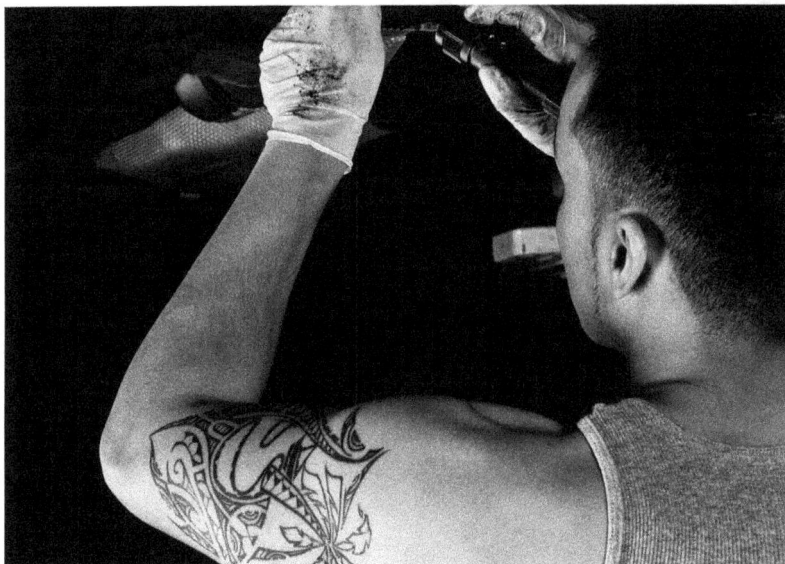

NASTY TO TRASHY/ ▪

If you are a real man, you have taken it one step further - to trashy. You have replaced your nice-guy tie with your wife-beater shirt. You are the boss. Commanding but not condescending, you show your raw sexual power. You are dirty, powerful, seductive and fucking amazing in bed.

There is no way you do it without being a bit psycho. If you have ever been to a White Trash house you know you'll inevitably find one door that has been bashed in. White Trash are not broken in like obedient house pets. They have a certain attitude that makes it all right to be daring, dominant and manic. There are no sexual constraints in their world. They gainfully earned their reputation of being White Trash through their direct indecent behavior. Proceed with caution is a freeway sign, not some subliminal message.

It is easy to be trashy in bed when you let yourself be a beast. After all, you have 97% of the same DNA as

apes. It is reasonable that you act like an animal at times. Though it does not mean you have permission to be an asswipe. Give your woman a voice, listen to her animal inside and fuck it like it wants. You may be pleasantly surprised how much of a freak she is in bed.

Once her freaky side starts to rear its head, ask her what she fantasizes about. Ask if she has ever been tied up or has tied anyone up. Once you get the feeling she is receptive to exploring a trashier sex life, let her know what you have in mind. Start to share some of your sexual fantasies. Come up with something you both have never tried so you can explore together.

One of the top three fantasies of women is safe rape.[1] If your woman is comfortable simulating a rape scene, you can do her a favor by playing it out.

First come up with a safe word like "poodle", which she can say if it gets to be too much. She has to know that if she says "poodle," you will stop no matter what. Once you establish a safety zone, it is time to crack her

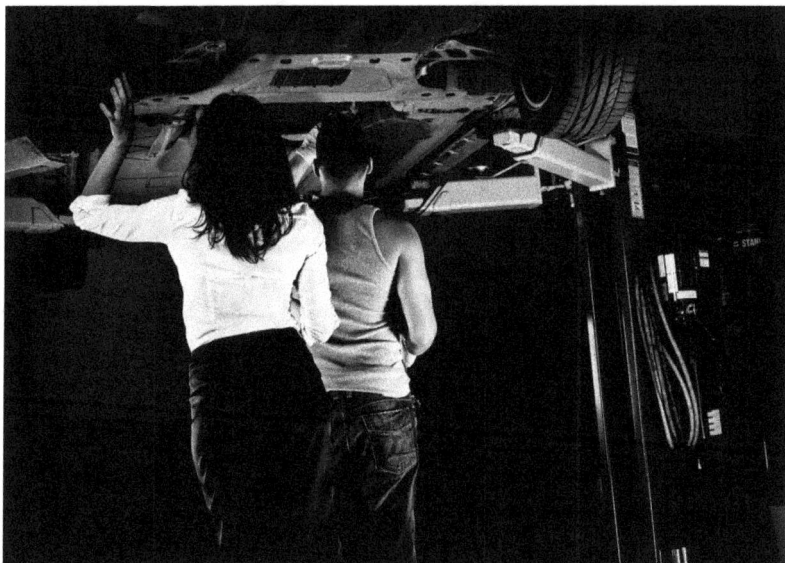

good-girl character and support her in exploring her love for violence. Her trashy side meeting yours for full-on mind-blowing sex.

It is a misconception that women aren't as violent as men. Amazons in Greek mythology were known to fight alongside men, slaying enemies and destroying cities. Through urbanization, women are losing touch with this part of themselves. Simulating a rape scene brings women back in touch with this instinctive fierceness. If your woman opens to the experience and lets go, she can rekindle feelings of being totally alive. A lot can be untwisted and stabilized through hard, rough sex. *Longer, Harder, Better.*

From 1973 through 2008, nine surveys of women's rape fantasies have been published. They show that about four in 10 women (31% to 57%) admit having rape fantasies with a median frequency of about once a month.[2]

FEMALE 28

" I hate to admit it but I lived a life of moderation
for far too long. Sure I let loose at times but
not really. I wanted to be more spontaneous but
ended up monitoring myself and others, judging
what was good and bad, right and wrong. This
made it hard to thoroughly enjoy anything. I
was never satisfied and falling into depression.
I sought the help of medicine and drugs then
ministers and healers. They didn't help. Nothing
did.

After years of solitude, I met this guy. He didn't
bullshit around. If he was angry, he would
express it. If he was happy, he was really happy.

He didn't hide anything, which forced me to face things I normally covered up, like rage, sadness and complete bliss.

After we had been hanging for a while he tried something with me. At first I wasn't sure about it. But once I got into it, it started to excite me.

Especially when I let him at it. I thought nothing could kick me out of my boredom and depression but this did: Rape.

Rape is what made me feel the best I had ever felt! All that I kept inside finally had a constructive way of expressing itself. I was on fire! I felt alive! I wanted more and more and more!!!!

To me, simulated rape is not about assault and intimidation. What it is about is losing control

over the little things. This guy did me a huge favor by dominating me. His intensity made it so I could experience my own. My buried desires started to reveal themselves and, all of a sudden, I started to feel amazing. The more violent the sex, the better I felt!

It wasn't that he acted like a complete monster. He made me feel safe and drew the line so I wouldn't run away. The times I clung onto fear, I could not reach the opening and benefits of the simulated rape scene. Then, he would ask that I stop controlling the situation and let go into his domination. OK. OK. Bam... something clicked into place. My body would loosen and a devilish grin would appear on my face.

The fun really started when I became a total submissive bitch. He could call me whatever he wanted and it was fine. He could do anything

to me and I loved it. You should see me now compared to years ago. My body language shows that I am ready to take on anything and everything. No one or nothing can get in my way. Since I've been having hard sex, I feel invincible.

There is no greater satisfaction than being fucked really hard over and over."

28 Marina del Rey, CA, U.S.A.

Start to talk to her like you are a stranger off the street.
Tell her she has a nice ass. Tell her she makes your dick
hard. Grab her by the neck and demand a kiss. Push her
around. Tell her how you want her to lick your swelling
dick. Move her head down. Grab her arms and keep
them behind her back and have her work on you. Then
turn her around. Pull her panties down and thrust your
dick into her from behind. Tell her that her behavior is
what made you rape her. Move her up against the wall.
Always have one hand on her to let her know she cannot
escape. If she starts to whimper, shut her up. Pull out
and make her masturbate in front of you. Have her look
you in the eyes and say you are a fucking warrior. Now
go down on her and suck her swollen clit. See to it that
she comes like the Mississippi River.

ONE MINUTE MAN/ ▪

Let's face it, if you are a one minute man something has got to change. And it can. There are guys who have moved from the premature ejaculation category to can't-get-it-down-if-I-try. Premature ejaculation rarely means you have a structural or physical problem. It is more an indication that the call of nature has a strong hold on you and that mother nature wants you to spread your seed and build an empire.

Men produce two hundred million sperm every day. These spermanators have one mission: to fertilize. If one can wiggle its way up to the big egg, they have succeeded as a whole. High five for the survivor. It is a hard fight.

You have millions of spermanators working their asses off to make sure you cum. It is thoughtful of them to be concerned about growing your empire but at one point you just have to stop listening to these suckers. You've got to see that your job is to pleasure a woman, not

impregnate her. Think of sex as an act of giving. Yes, manly man, you can be giving and still have a White Trash attitude. White Trash guys are as gentle and caring as they are rough.

Know that you are not solely responsible for how long you last and when you ejaculate. Sure you have a part in it, but it is the woman who holds the man's energy during sex.

The better your woman knows how to configure her energy to support yours, the more you both will get out of having sex together.

Think of yourself as a thin glass ball. If the ball is squeezed too tight, it will break into pieces. But when it is held just right, it keeps its form. On a purely energetic level, you are as fragile as a glass ball. This doesn't mean you are a wuss. It has nothing to do with physicality. What it means is that you are sensitive to the energetic exchange that happens in sex and need to be treated accordingly.

Prostitutes, as a whole, get this concept. Their energy is geared towards pleasing men. When a guy goes to a prostitute, he knows her time is all about him. He knows there will be no demands or expectations. He knows he can express himself however he wants without being judged. Prostitutes make themselves open for men to have a whole range of experiences.

That's why guys love them so much. To have someone for a whole hour who really cares for your sexual satisfaction is service at its best. (Pay them well.)

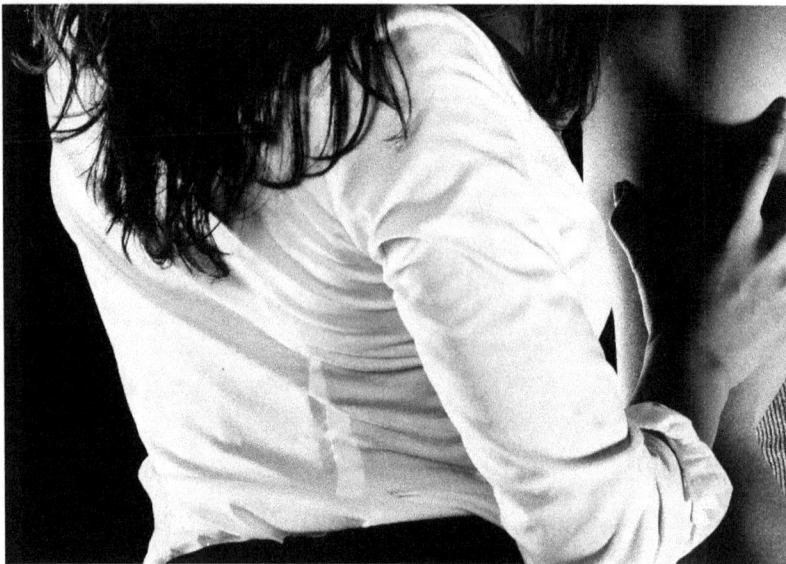

" I had a severe premature ejaculation (PE) problem. Each time I would attempt to have sex, I would come just by rubbing my penis on a vagina. I lasted about three seconds. In, out, in, ahhh, there it went.

Needless to say, after months of the same experience I became very frustrated. I really wanted to satisfy my girlfriend and couldn't.

Then one day, I found a book on how to treat PE. The content made so much sense. It addressed fast masturbation, how men learn by watching porn and how instant gratification can lead to PE.

I had to relearn how to masturbate by prolonging my pleasure and build sexual stamina by exercising my pubococcygeus (PC) muscle. Through systematic exercise, this muscle can be strengthened and subsequently can control ejaculation.

I was so excited that I started using the technique immediately. I practiced contracting the PC muscle between 30 and 45 minutes every morning (the book recommends 20 minutes per day). My penis became firmer and a bit larger.

Through these exercises, I learned how to masturbate without needing to ejaculate. According to the book and other resources, ejaculation costs a man his essential energies. By not coming and learning how to hold and spread into pleasure, men can reinforce their health,

longevity and clarity.

I have since trained my muscle to the point
where I don't come. My partner does and I keep
going. By resting every 20 to 30 minutes to let
my erection subside, the old blood in my penis is
replaced by fresh blood. This enables me to have
a fresh erection and continuous sex. The longest I
have gone with my partner is two hours.

Not everything went smoothly though. There
were times when I had jerks of uncontrollable
sensations which made me come. And often
I was so focused on the technique that I
disconnected from feeling, which upset my
partner. Connecting to my feelings while
maintaining control is what I now aim for.

Another very practical trick to make sex
smoother is going slow at the beginning,

screwing rather than thrusting, to avoid friction. Thrusting should happen only after the vagina is thoroughly lubricated. Of course, this doesn't mean that I only have slow sex. When her vagina is lubricated enough I can do just about anything, from a gentle screw to a forceful thrust. What I've noticed is that the greater the friction, the more chance of ejaculation.

I would lie if I said the secret was only in the technique. It's easy to think the technique will do everything. But it doesn't. These three steps made a difference to me: opening to my emotions, trusting my partner and being disciplined with the PC exercises. Additionally, I focus on giving to my partner rather than taking from her.

After a year and a half, I still practice the PC exercises, use lubricant and am fluid with my partner.

My favorite books for PE are:
  Master of Ejaculation by Gorden Lamb
  Multi-Orgasmic Man by Mantak Chia

There is hope for PE! It is possible to turn it upside down, from an embarrassing experience to mastering sexual power."

When you manage your energy appropriately, your sexual experiences are going to be

LONGER,
HARDER,
BETTER.

What does "appropriately" mean?

- It means feeling sensations in your whole body instead of solely focusing on the pleasure in your genitals.

- It means taking a break if you need to without being hard on yourself.

- It means letting go of being in charge and allowing your woman to hold you energetically.

- It also means not listening to spermanators, whose main goal is to get you to ejaculate.

Tips for

PREVENTING EJACULATION

1. Contract the muscle you use to stop the flow of urine. (This is the PC, or pubococcygeus, muscle.)

2. Take a deep breath.

3. Press the perineum, between the pubic symphysis and the coccyx, while contracting the muscle you use to stop urination.

4. Slow down.

5. Give oral sex, focusing your attention away from yourself.

6. If all else fails, stop. Take a cuddle break.

FEMALES ONLY

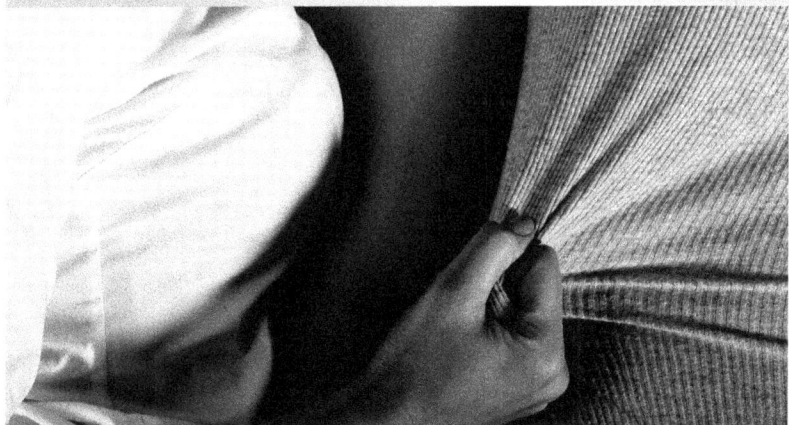

THINK PINK/ •

Pink. Moral, ethical and social implications of this color have been imprinted on you from the time you were born. Your gender has been identified by it. With this comes an expectation of how you are to be treated and should behave.

Parents, grandparents, teachers and friends approach you differently than they would if you were a guy. They use softer words, tone of voice, touch and references. You respond to them with laughter, a smile and maybe even a quick twirl of your hair. You were conditioned to get what you want based on these girly behaviors.

You have also been steered down a certain path, one that is not even close to that of your guy mates. A path that doesn't lead you to become an auto mechanic, firefighter or millwright. A path where you are expected to be nurturing and understanding or you are labeled a bitch. A path where you are judged on your attractiveness, niceness and ability to please others.

Greeting cards clearly feed into this delineation. Look at a card addressed to a guy and you will find words like "talented", "bright", "fantastic" and "wise." The font is less frilly and the colors are dark or cool. You never see a pink flower on a Father's Day card just as you don't run across a fishing rod on a Mother's Day card. Cards for females use words like "beautiful", "sweet", "precious" and "stylish." The messages to girls are completely different than those to guys.

The point is that gender roles are stamped into society and are blindly accepted as the truth. Things that are tolerable for women to do or be are not necessarily as accepted for men and vice versa.

Now this is fine if you are acting out of authenticity. But when you are stuck behaving the way society wants you to, there's a

Living outside the normality of an average woman makes you a gem. Cubic zirconia looks at you in envy. Diamonds want to be your best friend. You are not mass fabricated and it shows in the uniqueness of your personality and sexuality.

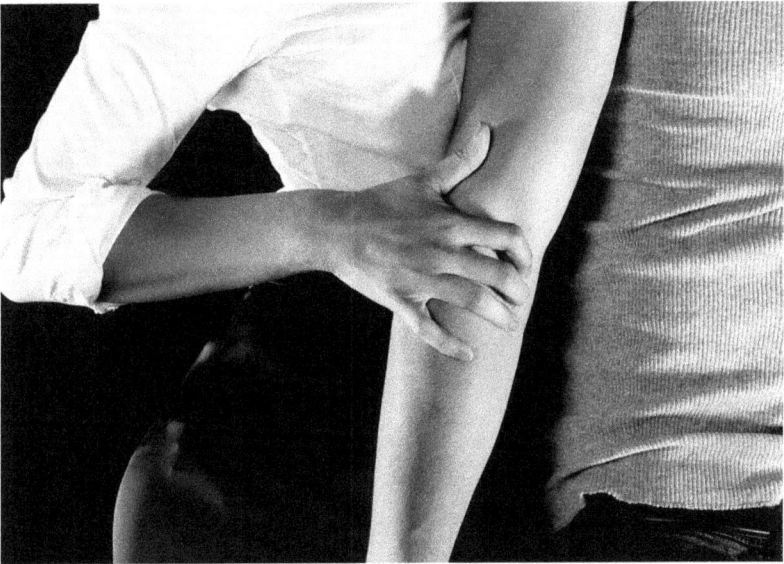

problem. You can't be yourself. And, you can't get what you want if you are hooked into the mentality of "that's the way things have always been." Follow the ways of society and you are as free as a puppet on the hand of a ventriloquist. Society talks through you. You are predictable, universal and, most strikingly, unsatisfied.

Who can be truly happy with society's hand up their butt?!

It may take cutting the apron strings to move towards what you want, just as Juliet did to try to reunite with Romeo. She sprung loose from society - her parents, nurse and social position in Verona - when she decided her loyalty and love for Romeo was her priority. Her determination made it so no one could get in the way of her decision to be with Romeo.

Those of you still living under your parents' roof, you are going to have a difficult time claiming authenticity when you are still feeding from the umbilical cord. Women (and men) who have freedom are by and large more sexual and accepting of getting into their trashy side. There is an authenticity that isn't present in unweaned adults.

Standing your ground and going for your desires despite the objection of others leads you towards authenticity and liberation. If you want to consciously use your pink power, you have to be aware of it.

Talk, dress and act like a woman and watch how men respond. Also watch how you respond. When you are dressed like a woman, men respond differently than if you were to wear army gear. You, too, act different. When you are dolled up you configure your energy in a different way. You walk, talk and flirt like a woman. You feel sexually attractive and can pull strings with this power. Every woman should be aware of this. If you are in the habit of wearing frumpy clothes, no makeup and/or workmen boots, you are not using your pink power. You are not sexually attractive to men when you act like one yourself.

I like wearing heels to work- makes me feel very hot.
8 hours ago

i know the feeling...
5 hours ago

I concur :)
2 hours ago

(from Facebook)

Even if you are not into dating men, start to find the balance between the part of you that kicks ass and the part that likes being a goddess. You, the ass-kicking goddess.

> " *There are only two types of women -*
> *goddesses*
> *&*
> *doormats.* "
>
> Pablo Picasso

WHEN A WOMAN BEHAVES LIKE A MAN, WHY DOES SHE BEHAVE LIKE A NICE MAN?

If you are the epitome of a girly girl, you too are not using your pink power. You may cleverly seduce people but most likely not from the part of you that is authentic. For you, the key is to drop the Barbie™ doll persona and get real. Stop acting dingy. Do something out of your ordinary girly routine. Break your well-manicured nails. Free yourself from proper Emily Post etiquette and act like White Trash.

The key is to balance Mars and Venus until you own the irresistible power that even a Roman god would fall for. It is more than just a psychological balance. It is an energetic configuration and an underlying

principle in understanding how you can have sex like White Trash. Simply put, it is a harmonization between high heels and hiking boots.

There must be an in-and-out through your states, behavior and clothing. This brings as much softness as toughness. If you are the kind of woman who is feminine but can also appear in boots, a plaid shirt and torn jeans to work your ass off all day, you understand the dance, lap dance in your case, between the two.

Think pink and your man will be at your feet begging for more. There is an irresistible urge to please a woman who is gentle yet powerful. Who is yin, mixed with a bit of yang. Who is a good girl with White Trash tendencies.

> The best lap dance is from the movie *Death Proof.* Check it out on YouTube.[3]

Good girls wait until marriage to have sex.
White Trash girls sleep with everything until marriage.

Good girls have high morals and standards.
White Trash girls are skanky and cheap.

Good girls wear conservative clothes.
White Trash girls dress like sluts.

Good girls act like ladies.
White Trash girls are obnoxious.

Good girls comply.
White Trash girls rebel.

**Good girls go to heaven.
White Trash girls go everywhere.**

POWER OF THE PUSSY/ •

Women, you have got to get it through your pretty little heads that you have the power. Men have a hard time admitting it but yes, you call all the shots. You say no, *he stops*. You say yes, *he goes*. You say maybe, *he waits*.

You make all the rules. If you do not want to have sex, the zipper is not going down. You can dangle a carrot in front of his nose, luring him towards your sexy thighs but unless you open the gate, he is getting nowhere close.

Even though women have the power, it is often covered by a veil of inhibition. For centuries women have been perceived as inferior to men. In 1840, Dr. John Elliotson stated in his book *Human Physiology*, "Woman is greatly inferior to man in reasoning powers, extent of use, originality, and grandeur of computation, as well as in corporeal strength. Women possess a small range of intelligence and less permanence of complexion, less consistency, impetuosity, courage, firmness of character except where affection subsists. She is more

disposed to believe all things compared to all persons, to adopt the opinions and habits of others, has no originality, but follows and imitates men."[1]

Dr. Elliottson would have a bullet in his head if he preached this same message today. However, there is something still lingering that alludes to the fact that women haven't stepped out of their position of inferiority. Feminist, refute this.

But it remains that a woman earns seventy-three cents for every dollar a man makes, the law labels pregnancy a "disability" and health insurance plans are more likely to cover Viagra® prescriptions than birth control pills.[2]

You don't need statistics to prove that women rest on a submissive role. Just look at your mom, her friends and their daughters. Their body language, voice, actions and decisions indicate that somewhere deep inside they still hold on to life as a bondservant. Your mom may boss your dad around to get him to do chores but power is not in telling a man what to do.

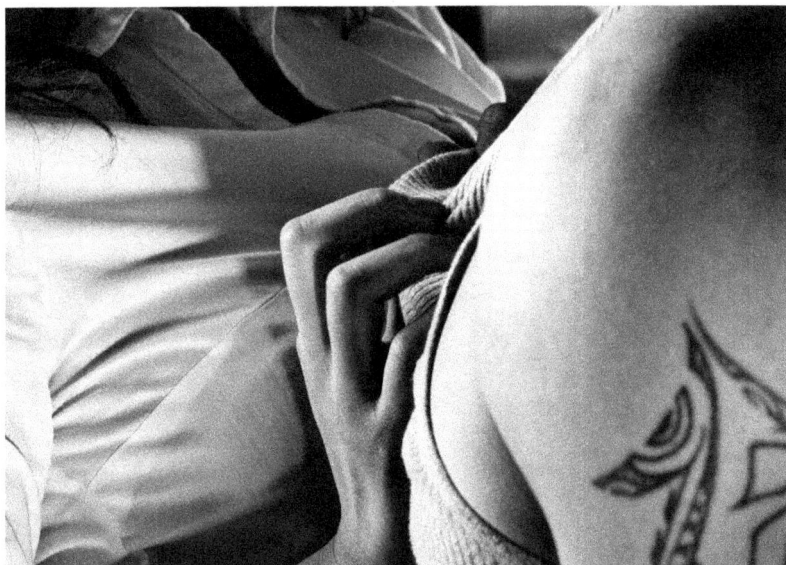

Expending your power does not mean you can change a man. Women often go into a relationship thinking that they can get their man to quit the habits they don't like. No one can change a person if the person does not want to change.

Real power is in the subtle way a woman configures her energy. As with all things energetic, this may not be directly noticeable. There are, however, typical signs that indicate whether a woman is using her real power. For example, a woman who moves with confidence and shows her command over a space is most likely expending her power. The opposite is a meek woman whom no one takes notice of. A woman who speaks with a grounded voice and attracts the respect of others is managing her power as opposed to little miss meek who can't even get the attention of her family's drop-kick dog.

The more a woman is in her power, the better she is at everything she does. Her predatorial nature keeps her on the top of the food chain. Women who own their power

embrace their fighter instinct like a queen bee battling for a colony or protecting her honey. They can stand up for themselves and make themselves heard. They are exacting and shrewd. *Business women. Mothers. Decision makers. CEOs. Teachers.* They say "*I can do that*" rather than "*That's a man's job.*" Nothing gets in their way of accomplishing what they want.

Athena, the goddess of war and wisdom, was a queen bee in her day. She was a fierce warrior skilled in strategy and warfare, excelling in activities traditionally associated with men. She also exhibited nurturing abilities. People in need called upon her motherly protection. Under her care, Odysseus and Heracles successfully accomplished their missions.

This goes to show that stepping into your power does not mean becoming a power-hungry bitch. Although taking that role for a while might be good for your development and liberation, it is certainly not necessary.

The key is in how you present yourself. People respect a woman who can say "*Yes!*" or "*No!*" and really mean it. When you stand your ground, you won't get pushed around. People don't question your decisions and trust in your leadership abilities.

---❈❈❈---

"I sensed that in Marilyn there was a certain amount of cunning as well as the innocence. I found her a fascinating mix. On one hand, she was vulnerable. But, on the other, calculating. She knew what she was doing, that one. There was never a false move with her."[3]

Johnny Hyde about Marilyn Monroe

---❈❈❈---

BOY TOYS/ •

When you exercise your power, the world is yours. People fall at your feet. You are a natural magnet and attract what you want. You just say the word and you'll be wined, dined and sixty-nined. There is no need for seeking dates online, getting lost in romance novels or resorting to a vibrator.

Look around at your female friends who have boy toys. They know how to use their power. They are always on the prowl, which makes them fun to be with. They are not the type that goes around complaining. Instead they go for what they want and love every moment. Samantha Jones from *Sex and the City* is a good example of a woman in this category. She is sexually confident. And she has always got a boy toy.

> 66 There isn't enough wall space in New York City to hang all of my exes. Let me tell you, a lot of them were hung.[1]

Samantha in *Sex and the City*

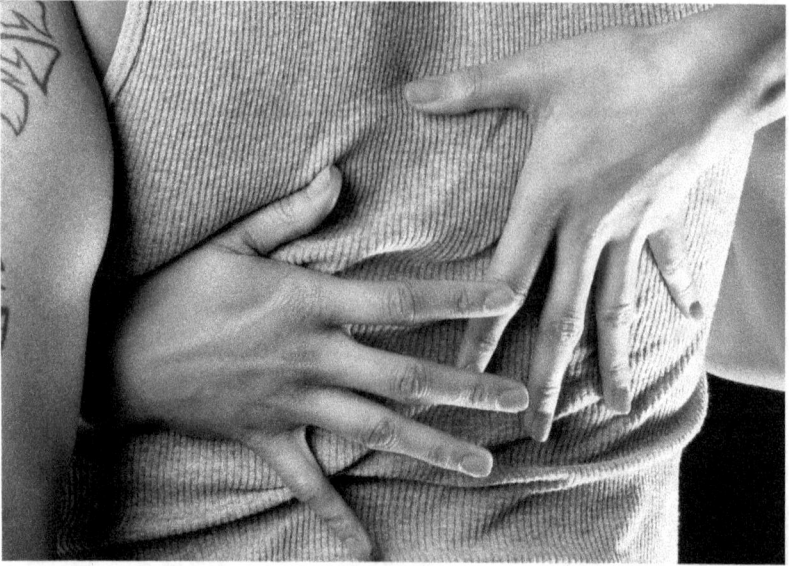

Samantha refers to herself as a try-sexual because she will try anything once. She goes from sleeping with one man to the next and is proud of it. Often women are called sluts for having too many one-night stands. When a man exhibits the same behavior he is considered a stallion. Why should women be less hungry for sex? Women have the same right to date, mate and fornicate.

Sex without strings is liberating. It comes with the same attitude as a righteous predator. When you put on your six-inch fuck-me pumps, you embody strength and determination to move forward and get what you want. The tiger in you goes straight for the kill. Nothing can stop you from ripping your teeth into fresh savory blood.

Boy toys are those you can prey on without any repercussions. You are free to do with them what you please. They are the confidence builders you need to know you can do anyone, anytime. Playing around with different men allows you to get to know yourself and what turns you on. Boy toys are mere stepping stones on the path to sexual freedom.

FEMALE

39

66 I grew up in a beautiful small country town with an unfortunately small-minded mentality.

As a teenager I tried to be well behaved there, aiming to keep a low profile lest the gossip monster raise its ugly head, yet inwardly I resented and pushed against the narrow local confines of acceptable behavior.

After I finished high school I moved to a big city for college — great excitement and a burgeoning sense of freedom finally giving wings to my inner rebel. Something deep inside me wanted to wake up, to stretch out, to know itself.

Some wild, free, deep power that had previously been politely caged wanted a stage to walk upon, to stride upon.

Sexual adventure became that stage. I became a night owl and several nights a week would go clubbing either by myself or with my friends, ostensibly to dance but in reality to flex this new power, to choose a young man as my prey for the evening, know I was going to have him, and either take him home to my place or go home to his.

I didn't want a boyfriend or emotional intimacy. Emotionally and personally I had little confidence, but the feeling of conquest and the intimacy of flesh against flesh were sweeter and more real than any conversation I could imagine. Slaking the thirst to experience and express the immensely satisfying power of the

sexual predator was what I was after. To spot a man across a room, relax into the depth of the animalistic part of me, and use it to pull him towards me... rrraowrr!!!

I never judged myself for that period, I feel like it was immensely important in my life, and now, almost 25 years later and with years of yoga and meditation under my belt, I recognise that power as a reserve of will, depth, juice, delight and health, that even now I aim to connect with and open to.

Sexual power is DELICIOUSLY GOOD FOR YOU!!"

39 Sydney, Australia

One of the definitions of a boy toy on urbandictionary. com is "A boy who will bend over backwards to do anything for a girl, knowing full well that the girl is using him."[2] Guys like to be taken advantage of sexually. Not having an emotional relationship is just as freeing for them as it is for females. Knowing there is not going to be a lifelong commitment, it is easy to let go. There is no need to conform to standards. If it doesn't work, either party can leave without trying to fix anything. Without a ball and chain, it is easy to flee when it's over.

Some relationships are only meant for the short term anyway. Anything longer than a fling would kill the spirit of both people. But many women fail to see that to get the maximum benefits, they need to have sex with different men. These women have an idealistic view of relationships, clinging onto fairytale dreams with happily-ever-after endings. They can't imagine a temporary relationship would ever lead to freedom. A mere shift in mentality and these women would see how much they can thrive from affairs.

Each man has something different to offer. One man may be good at oral sex while another may bring multiple orgasms simply by saying your name. And then there are those who fail in all areas. You never know unless you take him for a test drive.

> "Many people feel like a one-night stand is something to be ashamed of or embarrassed by. I disagree. There are many ways to get to know someone, and my personal favorite is seeing them naked in Happy Baby pose. I also feel it is important to have sex soon after meeting someone in order to find out if you have sexual chemistry together. Otherwise, you could wait two to three months after you start dating someone only to discover that your new boyfriend is bad in bed, or even worse, is into anal beads and duct tape."[3]
>
> Chelsea Handler in *My Horizontal Life*

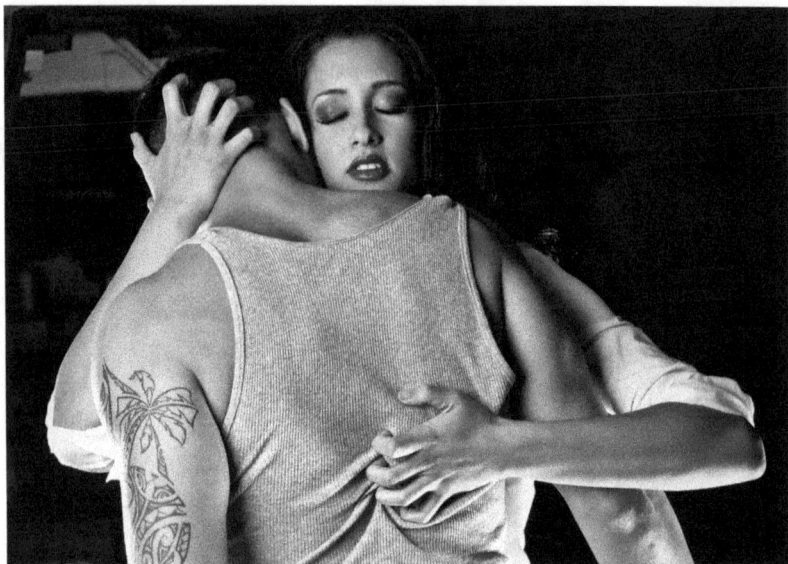

Once you have gained the confidence you need, accumulated enough notches in your belt and taken your share of men for a test drive, you can sanguinely go into a real relationship without any should-haves.

MOTHERPLUCKERS/ •

Sex and belly satisfaction. These are determining factors of whether or not a relationship is going to work. When you find someone your belly really resonates with, sex is going to be amazing! If the relationship successfully continues after the initial butterflies-in-the-stomach phase, you have something worth keeping.

Let's look at your enemy picture to learn what not to do when you find a keeper. Let's call your enemy Motherplucker and define her as a woman who drives her partner over the edge with demands and expectations.

Your enemy always wants something from her man and is often materialistic.

moth·er·pluck·er
[muhth-er-pluhk-er]
–noun
1. A woman who drives her partner over the edge with demands and expectations.

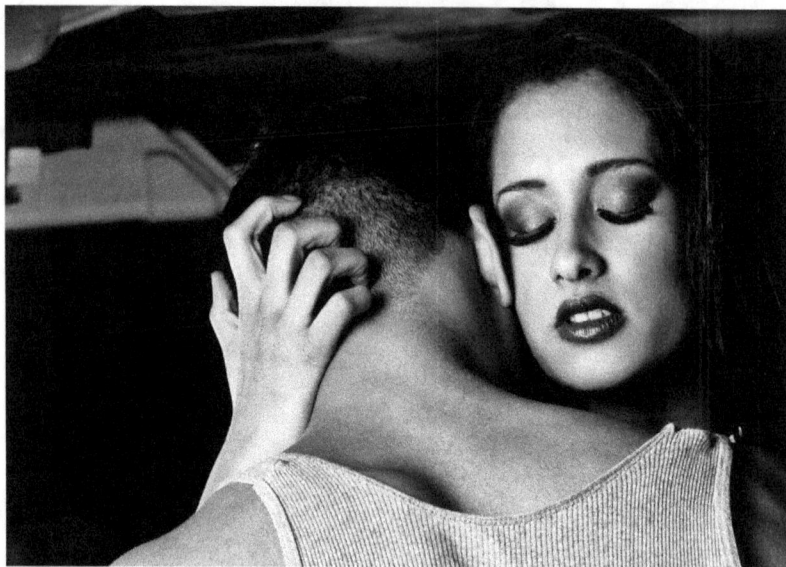

DO MOTHERPLUCKERS REALLY GET WHAT THEY NEED?

? DOES HAVING AN EXPENSIVE MASSAGE FROM A STRANGER REALLY SATISFY THEIR LONGING TO RUB AGAINST A LOVER?

DOES SHOPPING ON MILF LANE TAKE CARE OF THEIR LONGING LOINS? **?**

? DOES BITCHING TO THEIR BEST FRIEND FOR HOURS ON THE PHONE CALM THEIR FRUSTRATIONS?

DOES EATING A BOX OF CHOCOLATES FULFILL THEIR HUNGER? **?**

Yet the more she gets what she wants, the less she is satisfied with her life. You know her type well: She's a whiney princess with nothing between her perfectly plucked eyebrows but a set of shallow beliefs.

Motherplucker. She is the one who looks down on people for being openly sexual. Her do-gooder attitude kicks in when anyone around her strays from societal norms.

White Trash. A motherplucker abhors them. A motherplucker

couldn't be seen in a trashy place. All her trashy thoughts are pushed aside. Instead of talking about her fantasies, desires and lusts, she constantly bitches about all her problems, which inevitably stem from sexual frustration.

Yeah, her. The one who can solve her drama in one go — by having hot sex with her partner — yet suffers through life by being uptight and demand driven. Her demands bring her man to the brink of insanity. Does she not realize that in placing so many demands on her man, she pushes him away? Does she not see that her behavior can turn her man from a sex machine to a couch potato? Does she not recognize that her continued gripes can lead a guy to have problems getting it up?

Male sexual difficulties often arise from the pressures placed on him by his partner. When a guy turns his worries inside, he is often prompted by feelings of inadequacy and uselessness. This can cause him to lose his drive for sex. Ironically, a man who can't have an erection blames himself when it often has to do with his partner's behavior.

FEMALE **32**

    On our second date, he sheepishly admitted to not having had an erection for ten years. His marriage turned south after his kids were born and his wife became more and more demanding. Nothing he did made her happy. According to his recollection, he went from an enthusiastic fun-loving guy to a cold robot shortly after he withdrew from having sex with his wife. I didn't worry because I believed once he was with someone he felt comfortable around, his sexual desires would return.

The first night we had sex, he had trouble getting it up. I didn't make a big deal of it. The next

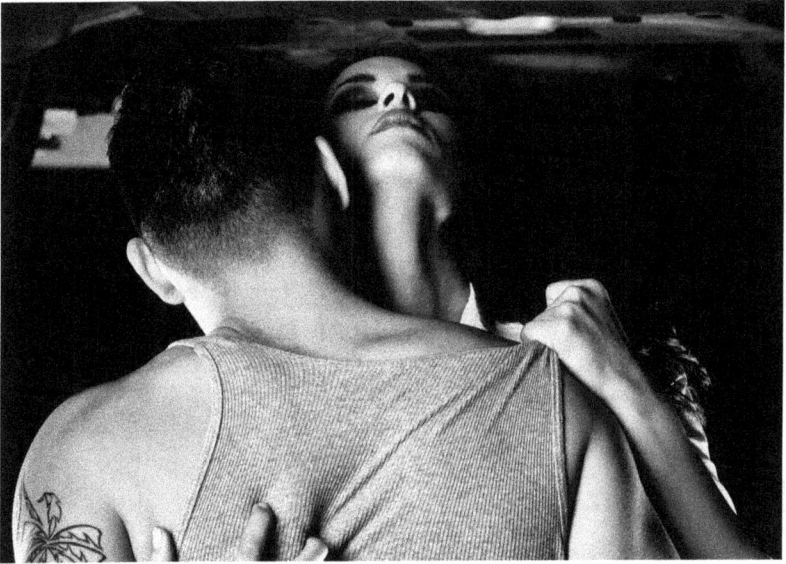

couple of times were the same. We would cuddle until we fell asleep. The more assured he felt around me, the more his excitement was being revived. Eventually he got back on track and now he is an unstoppable lovemaking machine."

32   Malibu, CA, U.S.A.

A woman is just as responsible for her partner's lack of sexual stamina as he is. A study performed in 2009 concluded that one in three men fear sex because of pushy partners.[1]

Although men act proud and tough, they still need praise, acknowledgement and support. Even the most manly man needs to hear how important he is and how he is cared for.

Women who nurture their man inevitably bring out the best in him. *Men want to be held.* Women who allow their man to have tantrums without getting wrapped up in them can be trusted. *Men want to freely express their aggression.* Women who drop grudges and appreciate their man in the moment are precious. *Men want to be regarded as honorable heroes.*

FEMALE

33

66 It's 10:19 pm. Mine is on his way home. He's been traveling all day. He just called and asked what I am wearing. I played coy and said I was working. I was already half dressed in a short office outfit. Why? Because he likes it.

A boyfriend... He is your king. He is a killer, a rapist, a terrorist. Let him be all that. Show him how to use his force, this wonderful, wild energy, this enthusiasm for life.

When I ask him what is important, he says: Her maturity. If she doesn't react at every little upheaval, even if he's done wrong, made mistakes

or forgotten her birthday. I say: Love the man
inside him, not the deeds he does or doesn't do.

He says: Let him have his fantasies, preferably
with you. I say: If he likes short skirts and
lipstick, wear them with a vampiness that would
make his mother blush.

He says: He is a little boy who wants to be loved.
I say: Enjoy all of him. His wild, uncontrolled
animal, his soft innocent boy, his warrior.

He says: Feed him. I say: Maybe I am over doing
this one. ;)

He says: Give him boundaries without scolding
him. I say: He needs to know where you stand
on things, clearly. If you are angry, wait.... until
there is quiet softness and time to tell him what
you like, not what you don't want him to do. Say

what you want in a gentle way and he will hear you.

He says: Laugh at his jokes, even if they aren't funny. I say: They are funny.

He says: Give him what he wants, often enough. I say: At times give him what he wants with an immediacy that will shock him..... if you're standing at the kitchen sink and he wants a hedgehog, give it to him without comment, wearing your washup gloves and all.

The most important thing of all is it is not your job to fix him, to alter him or to soften his edges. Your job is to love him, just as he is."

33 Dublin, Ireland

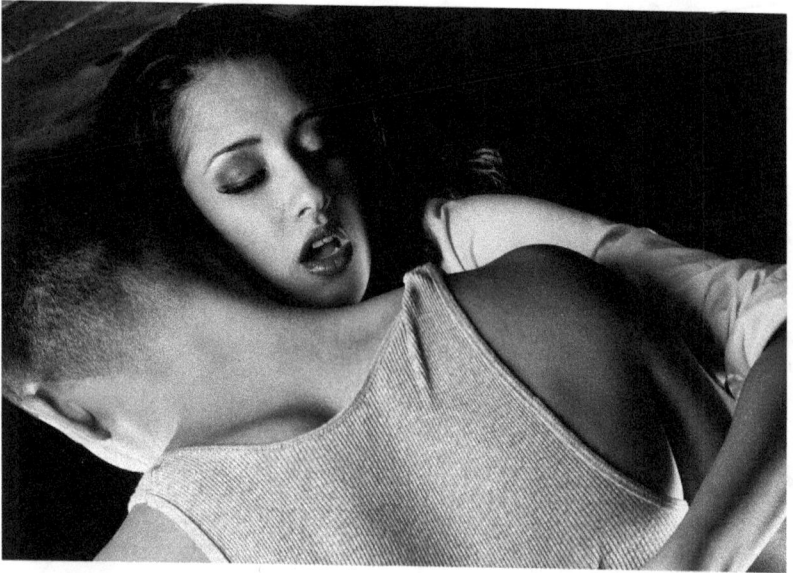

The modern-day woman is becoming more demanding and pushy. Coupled with the rising number of pluckers, there needs to be a conscious awareness of not placing too much pressure on men. It creates an imbalance in the predator-prey model when women kill what they actually need and want from men.

YOUR INNER WHORE/ •

There are motherpluckers and then there are real women. Women with passion. What makes the latter stand apart is that they tap into their sexuality and desires. They are not necessarily women who sleep around, though they might. What is true for them all is that they hold power, a feminine quality that resonates with intensity. You can say these types of women are totally in touch with their inner whore.

Women in touch with their inner whore are like Livia in Howard Bloom's book *The Lucifer Principle* in that they are womanly and seductive yet just as violent as men. Livia used her imperial power to get others to behead her rivals. Bloom writes, "Women encourage killers. They do it by falling in love with warriors and heroes. Men know it and respond with overwhelming enthusiasm. The Crusaders marched off to war with a lady's favor in their helmets. They were not setting out on some mission of gallant gentleness."[1]

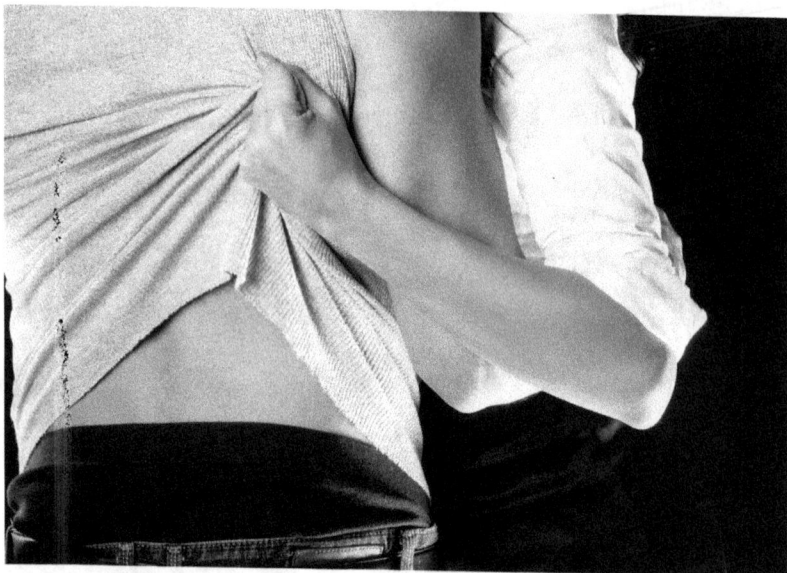

Greek mythology commonly paints the same picture of men fighting for women. The ancient Greeks believed the origin of war is a rivalry for women. Women know this and seduce men like Aphrodite at her strongest persuasive. Aphrodite is commonly depicted as having a conflicting female nature which combines seductive charm, physical beauty and a capacity for deception.

Women who tap from their inner whore have access to a wide spectrum, as they can go from being incredibly sensual to being as rough as sandpaper. If you are in touch with your inner whore, you are in touch with both your violence and your sensitivity. Anger, sweetness and everything in-between is what makes your inner whore tick.

Exploring your inner whore is like being a warrior who does not fit in to society and all its rules. Your inner whore is not meant for this world. It is strong when others are falling apart, promiscuous at the wrong times and creatively clever beyond people's normal realm of consciousness. When your inner whore is expressing itself

is when you need to pull from the White Trash part of yourself and not care what other people think of you, your ideas and your actions.

Once you are fully in touch with your inner whore, your life will be different. You will talk differently. You will resonate with different people. And, you will want different things. This may take you out of mainstream normality but will definitely give you the bang you are looking for.

For a man, it is a gift to be with a woman who is in touch with her inner whore. Look at how men respond to Samantha in *Sex and the City*. She is a woman who knows how to create a space for them to let go. They fall for her because she gives them room to express their sexual desires. After all, guys today are not much more advanced than cavemen. They want to reproduce, slay enemies and bring home the elk. It makes them feel powerful. Everything other than sex, war and eating does not matter much. When a woman demands something other than these three things, she fails to

address the essential part of a man - the mighty force which comes from the caveman inside. Trap this power and you go against nature, the man and yourself. Life will suck.

To satisfy a man, your inner whore must embrace his caveman. This means letting go of demands, expectations and judgments, which is exactly what prostitutes do and why guys go to them for sexual satisfaction.

Prostitutes do not place huge demands on their clients. They do not expect a guy to act like a family man. They do not judge a man for what he has or has not done in his life. They simply let a man be. (As long as he pays for it... All the more powerful to get this from someone he doesn't have to pay.)

Supporting your partner in discovering desires and having a partner that holds you in yours is huge. Desires are there whether or not you want to admit it.

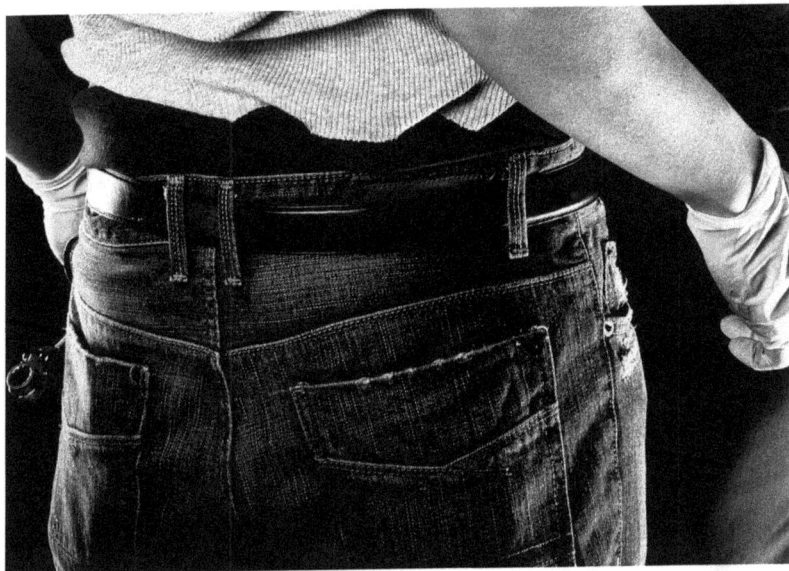

Addressing them can bring much satisfaction to your sex life.

When you start to match the desires of your man with those of your own, you can relate to each other more, which creates a feeling of closeness. Both of you feel understood.

This is when sex gets hot. It is when the daring, sarcastic, wild and sensual can come out. Leaving behind all relationship issues, you merge one force into another. Your man can let go into your watery qualities and you can be held by his fire and intensity. You balance one another out like yin and yang. In essence, this is what all people are looking for in a deep relationship.

GET IN TOUCH
WITH YOUR INNER WHORE

LANGUAGE: Direct

BODY: Proud

CLOTHES: Sexy

FRIENDS: Authentic

MONEY: Independent

SEX: Expressive

The inner whore doesn't have to do with a prostitute. It is a state of mind. When you are there, everything feels more alive. To get in touch with your inner whore, let go of social pretenses. Act like you are going to die tomorrow. Do things you want to do, not things that you feel you should. Keep a spare set of heels in your car. You never know where you'll end up when you follow your inner whore.

181/•

MALES & FEMALES

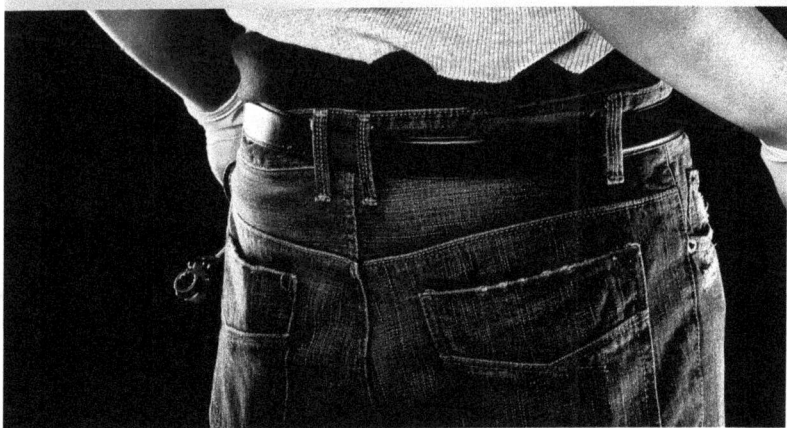

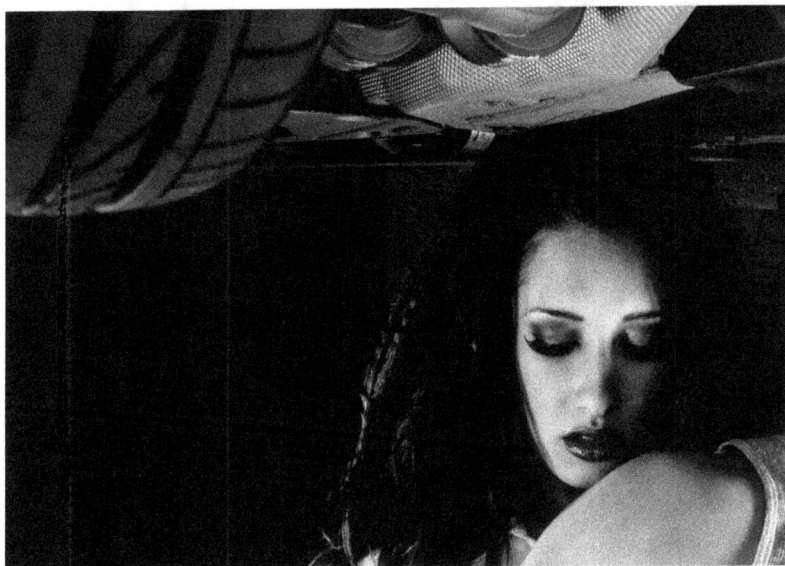

YOUR NEXT STEP/ •

When we strip down our belief systems, we are all the same. Leaving moral and ethical dilemmas aside, we have the same desires for sexual satisfaction. The force in us wants to procreate and kill our competition. It doesn't matter if our desires are channeled towards different expressions of material success, educational levels or destruction. In the end we are not much different.

Liberating our sexual desires gets us in touch with sensual parts of ourselves. It gets us in touch with spiritual dimensions of ourselves, even if some of you are not spiritual. It is the shortcut to inner freedom and saves us from drama and therapy. Solving life issues without being in touch with sexuality and desires does not work.

"YOU CAN'T HIDE FROM YOUR SHADOW."

Mickey in *Natural Born Killers*

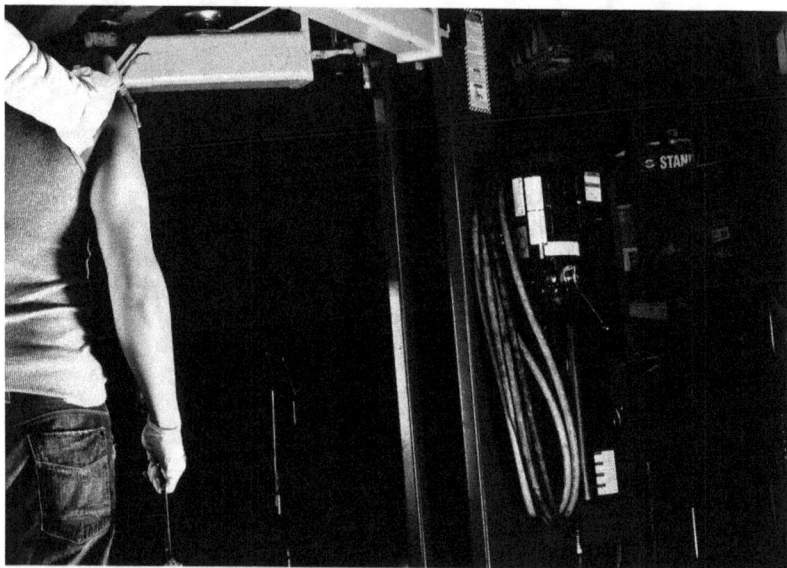

Sex is the foundation for success in the modern-day world. Integrating your inner White Trash core leads to a satisfaction which can't be easily achieved through the consumption of societal norms and goods.

There is no way out. You can't bypass your sex drive and play nice. Just look around at neighbors, coworkers and family members. Most are caught up in a prefabricated self-delusion. They don't get what they want and you can feel it.

The good thing is that now people can freely express themselves. Fifty years ago guys would have gone to a prostitute for a good blow job and now they get it as a standard from every partner. And women are much more independent, choosing partners without being made outcasts.

The question is:

ARE YOU

FRUSTRATED

ENOUGH?

Without frustration, you won't change a single thing. How do you know if you are frustrated? Ask yourself, do you have sex at least once a day? When you see a passionate sex scene in a movie, can you relate to it? Do you have moments of deep intimacy and feelings

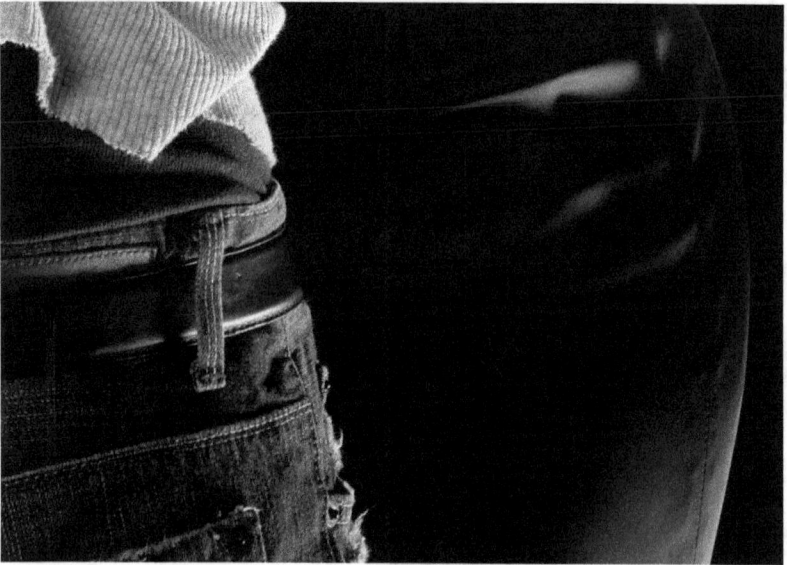

of uncontrollable desire? Is your partner sexually interested in you? Do you desire your partner? Are you still sexually attractive?

If you lean towards any signs of frustration and wonder where to go from here, why not live out your White Trash side. Make freaky a part of your everyday life:

BE THE BOSS. If you aren't the boss at work or at home, take on a role where you can make decisions and claim alpha status.

DO SOMETHING PHYSICAL. Dig a ditch, take Flamenco lessons, hold a yoga pose for more than one hour, put on boxing gloves and hit something. Be active. Exercise activates the nervous system and pumps blood to the genital region. It also gets you into your belly.

WRITE DOWN TEN THINGS YOU FEAR AND DO THEM. Have one of your friends hold you accountable.

LIVE OUT YOUR FANTASIES. Don't just keep them in your head. Ask to be dominated, raped or tickled. Buy sex toys if they help you get into the wild animal that doesn't stop.

GO TO A KINKY BAR. Meet people in person who are just as freaky as you. Online forums do not count. You have to get out there and talk to real people who have desires that are just as slutty as yours.

CHOOSE AN ANIMAL AND HAVE SEX LIKE IT. Bark, roar or meow. Lick, bite and roll. Do things that the animal would do. Be playful.

HAVE WHITE TRASH WEDNESDAYS. Smell like gasoline, cigarettes and cheap perfume. Play the part. Walk it. Talk it. Be it.

GO TO A WHITE TRASH EVENT. Go to a WWC, Nascar or tattoo convention. Be an asshole if your fighter or car is not beating the others.

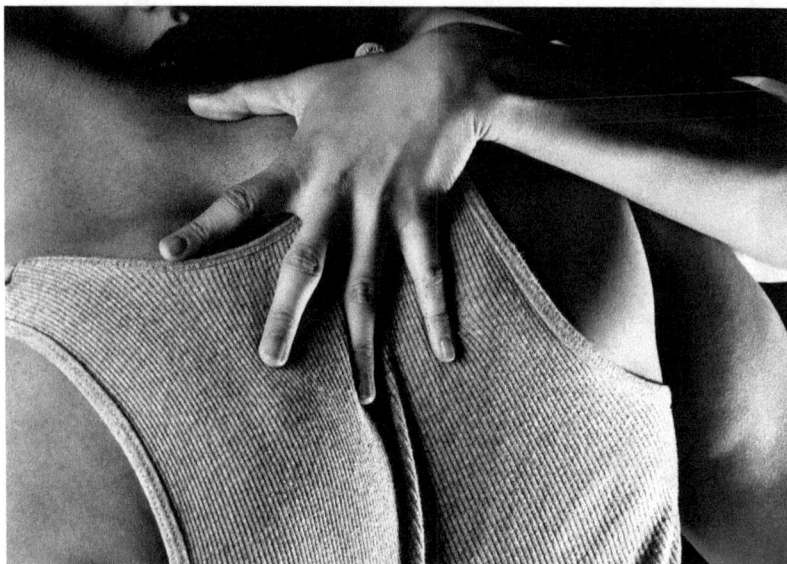

GO FOR WHAT YOU WANT. This always puts you in resonance with people and potential partners who are likely to make you feel really good.

DON'T BE ATTACHED TO WHO YOU THINK YOU ARE. The path to liberation means stepping outside your normal patterns and making your life rock.

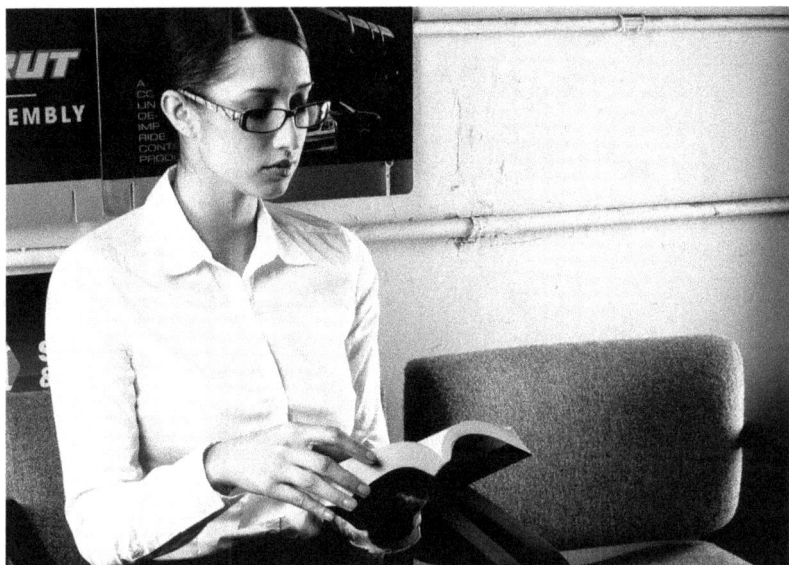

"

We can spend our lives letting
the world tell us who we are.
Sane or insane. Saints or sex
addicts. Heroes or victims. Letting
history tell us how good or bad
we are. Letting our past decide
our future. Or we can decide for
ourselves. And maybe it's our job
to invent something better.

Chuck Palahniuk

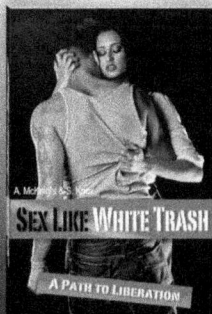

CHECK US OUT/●

Visit our website:
www.sexlikewhitetrash.com

Become our Facebook fan:
www.facebook.com/likewhitetrash

Follow us on Twitter:
www.twitter.com/likewhitetrash

Buy a "Longer, Harder, Better" t-shirt:
www.zazzle.com/likewhitetrash

REFERENCES/•

Intro
1. Americans Rate Sexual Satisfaction Low, Report Desire For More Pleasure According to New Trojan® Survey. Trojan. July 1, 2009. <http://www.trojancondoms.com/ArticleDetails.aspx?ArticleId=20>

Awaken the Force
1. Tyson. Dir. James Tobak. Fyodor Productions, 2009. DVD. ("My power is...")
2. Dangerous Beauty. Dir. Marshall Herskovitz. Regency Enterprises, 1998. DVD. ("It's the wanting that keeps us alive.")
3. Palahniuk, Chuck. Fight Club. New York: W.W. Norton & Company, 1996. ("You aren't alive anywhere like you're alive at Fight Club...")

Multi-Culti
1. Brenner, Robin. Understanding Manga and Anime. Connecticut: Libraries Unlimited, 2007.

2. Herdt, Gilbert. Guardians of the Flutes, Vol. 1.
Chicago: University of Chicago Press, 1994.
3. Fight Club. Dir. David Fincher. 20th Century Fox,
1999. DVD.
4. Cloud, John. "Bondage Unbound." Time Magazine
January 19, 2004. <http://www.time.com/time/2004/sex/
article/bondage_unbound_growing01a.html>
5. < http://www.quotationspage.com/quote/117.
html > ("Puritanism: The haunting fear that someone,
somewhere is having a good time.")

Sin-sational

1. Kahr, Brett. Who's Been Sleeping in Your Head? The
Secret World of Sexual Fantasies.   New York: Basic
Books, 2008.
2. Angelina Jolie - Inside Actors Studio Part 1. Host
James Lipton. New School University, February 2009.
<http://www.youtube.com/watch?v=kH_6Fu3j3Q0>
3. AskMen Contributor. "Exploring Female Sexual
Fantasies."<http://www.askmen.com/dating/
vanessa_100/120_love_secrets.html>

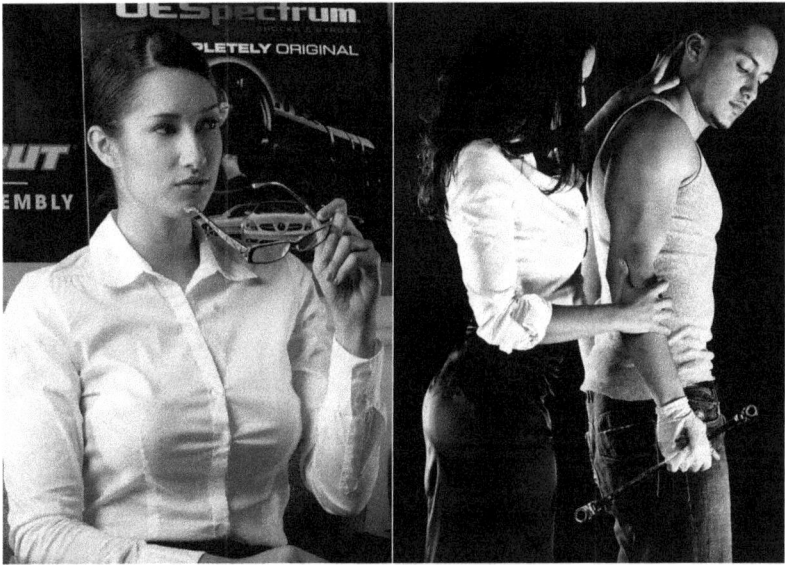

4. Friday, Nancy. <u>My Secret Garden</u>. New York: Pocket Books, 2001.

5. "Sexes: Male Fantasies" <u>Time Magazine</u> February 18, 1980. <http://www.time.com/time/magazine/article/0,9171,921829,00.html>

6. <u>Secretary</u>. Dir. Steven Shainberg. Slough Pond, 2002. DVD.

7. <u>Californication</u>. Dir. Stephen Hopkins. Showtime, 2007.

Sexcess

1. <u>Wall Street</u>. Dir. Oliver Stone. 20th Century Fox, 1987. DVD.

2. <http://www.dictionary.com>

3. <u>The Matrix</u>. Writ., dir. and prod. Andy Wachowski and Lana Wachowski. Groucho II Film Partnership, 1999. DVD.

4. funnyoneliners. January 14, 2011 <www.twitter.com/funnyoneliners>

5. Hill, Napoleon. <u>Think and Grow Rich</u>. New York: Soho Books, 1937.

6. Cawthorne, Nigel. <u>Sordid Sex Lives</u>. London: Quercus Books, 2010.

Uncensored Creativity
1. <http://quotationsbook.com/quote/25117/#axzz1H1NnpZsS> ("No great genius has ever existed without some touch of madness.")
2. <http://www.yummy-quotes.com/marie-curie-quotes.html> ("We must act.")
3. Fisher, Helen. "Why Love Can Make You More Creative." O The Oprah Magazine February 2010. <http://www.cnn.com/2010/LIVING/personal/02/10/o.love.makes.you.creative/index.html>
4. Handwerk, Brian. "Artists Have More Sexual Partners, U.K. Survey Hints." National Geographic December 2005. <http://news.nationalgeographic.com/news/2005/12/1215_051215_creative_sex.html>
5. <http://thinkexist.com/quotation/making_the_simple_complicated_is_commonplace/201908.html> ("Making the simple complicated is...")

Kitchen Quickie
1. <http://www.textsfromlastnight.com>
2. Esquivel, Laura. Like Water for Chocolate. New York: Doubleday, 1989.

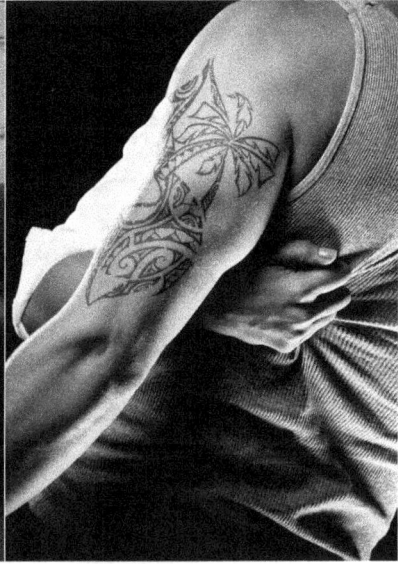

3. <u>Ramen Girl.</u> Dir. Robert Allan Ackerman. Media 8 Entertainment, 2008. DVD.
4. <http://www.metrolyrics.com/r-kelly-lyrics.html>

Fighting & Fucking
1. Palahniuk, Chuck. <u>Fight Club</u>. New York: W.W. Norton & Company, 1996.
2. New Oxford American Dictionary, 2nd Edition (2005).
3. <u>Tyson</u>. Dir. James Tobak. Fyodor Productions, 2009. DVD.
4. <u>A History of Violence</u>. Dir. David Cronenberg. New Line Cinema, 2005. DVD
5. <http://www.violence.de/> ("Cultures that repress sexuality...")
6. Yong, Ed. "Shedding light on sex and violence in the brain." <u>Discover</u>. February 9, 2011.

Stain the Sheets
1. <u>Along Came Polly.</u> Dir. John Hamburg. Jersey Films, 2004. DVD. <http://www.youtube.com/watch?v=xDnVl44FVhs>
2. Austen, Jane. <u>Pride and Prejudice</u>. New York:

Tribeca Books, 2010.
3. TwoTurntablesNMic, 2010. <http://www.youtube.com/watch?v=r2PM0om2El8>
4. B52s. "Love Shack." Cosmic Thing. Warner Brothers, 1989.

Smell Like a Man
1. Brad, Steve. "Pheromones in Male Perspiration Reduce Women's Tension, Alter Hormone Response that Regulates Menstrual Cycle." Penn News March 14, 2003. <http://www.upenn.edu/pennnews/news/pheromones-male-perspiration-reduce-womens-tension-alter-hormone-response-regulates-menstrual-c>
2. Russell, MJ. "Olfactory Influences on the Human Menstrual Cycle." Pharmacol Biochem Behavior. November 1980.
3. <http://www.pheromonesattract.net>

Flying Solo
1. <http://en.wikiquote.org/wiki/Woody_Allen> ("Don't knock masturbation...")
2. Treptow, Cornelia. "U.K. Government Encourages

Teen Masturbation?" <u>ABC News</u> July 14, 2009.
<http://abcnews.go.com/Health/MindMoodNews/
story?id=8072314&page=1>
3. Marnia. "Sex may keep stress at bay." <u>Reuniting Healing</u>
<u>with Sexual Relationships</u>. January 2006. <http://www.
reuniting.info/science/articles/sex_calms_nerves_before_
public_speaking>

Hunting for a Keeper
1. <http://www.textsfromlastnight.com>

Overstimulation
1. AFP. "US Internet Users Staying Connected During Sex:
Study." <u>Google News</u> September 15, 2010.
<http://www.google.com/hostednews/afp/article/
ALeqM5ibd-fK7uWauc_vZwTzvuyU82lMQQ>
2. <u>Married with Children</u>. Dir. Ron Leavitt. 1987. <http://
www.imdb.com/title/tt0092400/quotes>

Pulls of Nature
1. Chang, Stephen, Dr. <u>The Tao of Sexology</u>. San
Francisco: Tao Publishing, 1988.

2. <u>Full Body Orgasms: Fact or Fiction</u>. Shine from Yahoo. May 13, 2010 <http://shine.yahoo.com/channel/sex/full-body-orgasms-fact-or-fiction-1439032>

Chick with a Dick
1. Strauss, Neil. <u>The Game</u>. New York: Regan Books, 2005.
2. Donovan. "Interview with Neil Strauss Author of 'The Game.'" <u>The Attraction Chronicles</u>. September 9, 2005. <http://attraction-chronicles.blogspot.com/2005/09/interview-with-neil-strauss-author-of.html>

Nice to Nasty
1. Deida, David. <u>The Way of the Superior Man</u>. Boulder: Sounds True, 2004.

Nasty to Trashy
1. Cox, Tracey. "Living Out the Top 3 Female Fantasies." <u>iVillage</u> September 2, 2005.
2. Castleman, Michael. "Women's Rape Fantasies: How Common? What Do They Mean?" <u>Psychology Today</u> January 14, 2010.

Think Pink
1. <http://www.facebook.com>
2. <http://thinkexist.com/quotation/there_are_only_two_types_of_women-goddesses_and/168486.html> ("There are only two types of women...")
3. <u>Death Proof</u>. Dir. Quentin Tarantino. Dimension Films, 2007. DVD.
or anna120576. Death Proof Lap Dance Scene. October 2010. <http://www.youtube.com/watch?v=F26dDWNM1kQ>
4. <http://www.twitter.com/robdelaney>

Power of the Pussy
1. Elliotson, John. <u>Human Physiology</u>. Charleston: Nabu Press, 1840.
2. Wiehl, Lis. <u>The 51% Minority: How Women Still Are Not Equal and What You Can Do About It</u>. New York: Ballantine Books, 2007.
3. Taraborrelli, J. Randy. <u>The Secret Life of Marilyn Monroe</u>. New York: Grand Central Publishing, 2009.

Boy Toys
1. <u>Sex and the City</u>. Creator Darren Star. HBO, 1998.

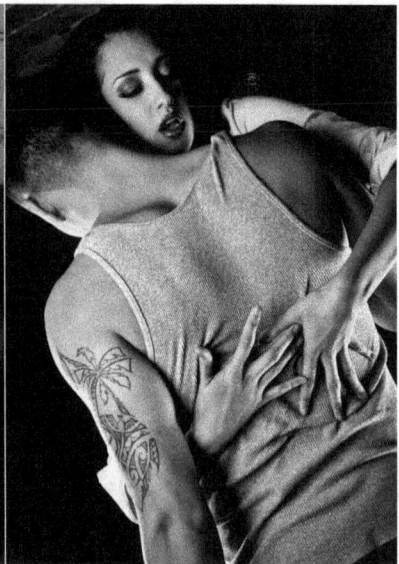

<http://www.imdb.com/title/tt0159206/quotes>
2. <http://www.urbandictionary.com>
3. Handler, Chelsea. <u>My Horizontal Life: A Collection of One-Night Stands</u>. New York: Bloomsbury, 2005.

Motherpluckers
1. Aruna. "One In Three Men Fear Sex Because of 'Demanding Wives.'" <u>Med India</u>. June 20, 2009. <http://www.medindia.net/news/One-In-Three-Men-Fear-Sex-Because-Of-Demanding-Wives-53222-1.htm>

Your Inner Whore
1. Bloom, Howard. <u>The Lucifer Principle: A Scientific Expedition into the Forces of History</u>. New York: The Atlantic Monthly Press, 1995.

Your Next Step
1. <u>Natural Born Killers</u>. Dir. Oliver Stone. Warner Bros. Pictures, 1994. ("You can't hide from your shadow.")

X Made with total Dedication
        & belly Love!

O Now go and get the sex you want!!!

www.ingramcontent.com/pod-product-compliance
Lightning Source LLC
Chambersburg PA
CBHW060843280326
41934CB00007B/900